Praise for
Bodywise: weaving somatic psychotherapy
and the Buddha in everyday life:

"It's so good to have these pieces collected in one place, so that we can clearly see their value, and feel gratitude for Kamalamani's wisdom, wit, common sense, deep knowledge of Buddhism, and enormous generosity of spirit. I have always felt that Buddhism, especially Vajrayana, has a profound connection with body psychotherapy; and it is a great pleasure for example to read Kamalamani on Green Tara - a figure of personal meaning to me - and her development of Shunryu Suzuki's brilliant slice through mind-body dualism: 'Our body and mind are not two and not one.... Our body and mind are both two and one'. This book will be of great help to anyone interested in body psychotherapy, in Buddhism, and in ecopsychology, or in the relationship between the three."

- Nick Totton, Body psychotherapist, trainer and author of *Embodied Relating: the Ground of Psychotherapy*

"Her heart and mind are open to the world, allowing it in and herself to live outwardly with compassion and love."

- Nancy Eichhorn, Founding Editor-in-Chief of *Somatic Psychotherapy Today*

Bodywise

weaving somatic psychotherapy, ecodharma and the Buddha in everyday life

Other books by Kamalamani

Meditating with Character (2012) published by Mantra Books.

Other than Mother: Choosing Childlessness with Life in Mind (2016) published by Earth Books.

Bodywise

weaving somatic psychotherapy,
ecodharma and the
Buddha in everyday life

by Kamalamani

Somatic Psychotherapy Today
Trending Somatic Practices Influencing Our Field Today

Copyright information

Each of these articles were published previously in *Somatic Psychotherapy Today* between Fall 2012 and Spring 2017. *Somatic Psychotherapy Today* is an independent international publication that is validated by professional organizations and associations representing various modalities in the fields of body psychotherapy, somatic psychology, and pre-natal and peri-natal psychology. For further information: www.somaticpsychotherapytoday.com

Copyright © Kamalamani 2017

ISBN: 9781549934117

Kamalamani has asserted her right under the Copyright, Designs and Patents Act 1988 to be identified as the author of this work.

This book is copyright material and must not be copied, reproduced, transferred, distributed, leased, licensed or publically performed or used in any way except as specifically permitted in writing by the publishers, as allowed under the terms and conditions under which is was purchased or as strictly permitted by applicable copyright law. Any unauthorized distribution or use of this text may be a direct infringement of the author's and publisher's rights and those responsible may be liable in law accordingly.

A CIP catalogue record for this book is available from the British Library.

Contents

Foreword 1
Preface 5

1. Green Tara's Apprentice 9
2. Wild Horses and Olympic Dreaming 16
3. Touched by the Past in the Present 21
4. Mammal Body 26
5. Holding to Nothing Whatever 32
6. Diagnosing 38
7. The Body Politic 43
8. Consuming passions 48
9. Sheer Coincidences? 54
10. Meditating with Character 59
11. The Burning House 65
12. Terrorized Bodies 72
13. Diversity 77
14. All at Sea 83

"The task of the bodhisattva is to do the best one can, without knowing what the consequences will be. Have we already passed ecological tipping-points and civilization as we know it is doomed? Frankly, we don't know – yet rather than be overawed by the unknown, the bodhisattva embraces "don't know" mind, because Buddhist practice opens us up to the awesome mystery of an impermanent world where everything is changing whether or not we notice…if we do not really know what's happening, do we really know what's possible, until we try?"

- David Loy, *A New Buddhist Path: Enlightenment, Evolution and Ethics in the Modern World*

Foreword

Kamalamani's initial 2012 column introduced an intimate look at a Buddhist perspective in body psychotherapy to our readers at *Somatic Psychotherapy Today*. We were invited into an awareness of all sentient life and living processes; her writings encouraged personal reflection and professional consideration.

Over the past five years, Kamalamani has shared and thankfully continues to share life at the confluence of body psychotherapy, ecopsychology, Buddhism and narrative in Bristol, UK in her regular *Bodywise* articles. She explains that her work with clients in relational and embodied ways continually deepens her own bodily awareness and Buddhist life and training—she's been a practicing Buddhist since her early 20s and was ordained in 2005. She calls herself a therapist but this label in fact expands into a medley of roles. She's a "midwife, witness, confident, mentor, teacher, sounding board, and, as the transference [with clients] develops, a provisional mother, father, brother, sister, daughter, son, lover and Fairy godmother and enlightened being" (from 'Diagnosing' – see chapter 6).

Many writers share their work from a distance; there's a keen third person feel to the text. You hear their voice but it's only that, a voice. Yes, I Kamalamani's British accent loud and clear and love every intonation and syllabication; and yet, I feel her, too. Her core presence resonates within carefully selected details, quotes, sutras, and artwork that accompany her stories. She offers readers insight and enlightenment through personal and clinical anecdotes that range from birth to death, from meditating with character to Reich's character structures, from trauma and terrorized bodies to diversity and more. She offers more questions than answers. There's space for opening and sensing, time to quietly be with oneself and time to join forces with our global community and feel the outrage, the love, the fear, the bliss that comes with interaction.

I look forward to reading her columns. Her tone is warm, immediate, accessible. Her writing skills honed, professional, expansive; her articles require little to no editing. I simply sit back and experience what came to her mind when the issue's theme was announced, what reflections found their way to the final draft. I marvel at the complexity woven within simple words and phrases, how she incorporates other people's words into her foundation, as she builds a solid structure to support the point (or points) she is focused on. There is never a dull moment, never a dead zone in terms of how the article reads; her voice carries me line-by-line as I anticipate where she might go, appreciate when I am right and curious when I guess wrong and find myself somewhere completely unfamiliar, intrigued by the content, the twists and turns that brought me to this new and often sacred space.

When she shared her first book, *Meditating with Character*, I developed a deeper understanding of her work, how she explores and helps others to explore interconnections inwardly. She writes that by "tapping into our connection with our body-mind in meditation, we enter the realm of embodiment". By embodiment, she means "the sense we make of being present with a body-mind." I reviewed her second book, *Other Than Mother: Choosing Childlessness with Life in Mind*, with mixed feelings. Her choices felt clear, conscious, known, based on what she knew she wanted and why. Yet, her position triggered personal memories of my past, of choices made and those made for me, of children conceived but never brought to life. It was a healing read, a delicate review to write, a balance of her story and my own.

I find this same sense of equanimity in all of Kamalamani's writing. Even when writing about fear and terror while in Paris during the 2015 ISIL attack, her reflection comes from a place of mental calmness and presence, of composure and even temper. She shares a story without judgement, there's no value assigned, no good or bad, right or wrong, there is simply her experience and what she makes of it, where it takes her today and where it might lead her tomorrow. She is not one to stay stuck, to allow a sedentary attitude to prevail. Her heart and mind are open to the world, allowing it in and herself to live outwardly with compassion and love.

This book comes from this place of gratitude and graciousness. Kamalamani offered to create an e-book of all her columns and to donate proceeds above the cost of creation and publication to *Somatic Psychotherapy Today*, to help defray the costs associated with an independently run international magazine. It is from generous gifts like Kamalamani's and others who donate to SPT that we continue to exist.

With gratitude,

Nancy Eichhorn, PhD
Founding Editor-in-Chief, *Somatic Psychotherapy Today*
www.SomaticPsychotherapyToday.com
September 2017

Preface

When I was in further therapy training as an Embodied-Relational therapist I remember happening upon Nick Totton, my then teacher – now friend and colleague, too – reading one of his books. He had bought a pile of them along to the training residential for us students to read. I smiled, I hadn't authored any books back then, but imagined my satisfaction if I had, browsing my finished work. Our eyes met. "It's like reading my diary," he said, smiled, closed the book, and wandered off.

Re-reading *Bodywise* in readiness for its production puts me in my mind of this interaction with Nick many years ago. Reading the columns I have written for *Somatic Psychotherapy Today* this past five years is rather like reading my diary. My initial writing brief for my first *Bodywise* article was to say something about my work from 'across the pond' as many contributors are based in the States. 'Brief' sounds rather chilly and formal. The reality was a warm invitation from Nancy Eichhorn, the founding Editor-in-Chief, to reflect on my current work as a body psychotherapist, my practice of Buddhism, and my work as an ecopsychologist, and then to write about it. So I did, associating as best I could the work with which I was currently engaged with the theme of each edition of *Somatic Psychotherapy Today*. It was an enjoyable challenge and the themes were many and varied; from diversity, diagnosis, and trauma to pre and perinatal psychology, embodied spirituality and societal embodiment and disembodiment.

This work is akin to reading my diary as it reminds me of how I was and what I was up to at the time of writing each of these pieces - as well as the odd moment of thinking "wow, I wouldn't write that now!" (The Buddha was definitely on to something when he kept going on about impermanence!) It also reminds me of the events shaping my work, from recollecting the losses and celebrations of friends through to world events of the past and present. Recalling this, the image of a bubbling cauldron comes to mind. I am struck afresh by how the therapeutic relationship is shaped by rich ingredients from all realms of life; from the personal to the global, the political, economic, ecological, social, transpersonal – it's all in there. Our animal bodies; our energetic bodies; our intellectual bodies; our feeling bodies. Our passionate bits and ambivalent bits. As two humans meet as client and therapist in that moment in time, all the meetings and encounters we have ever had also meet, in a sense, as we move in and out of contact, doing the work. Maybe this is amplified even more in working with an active awareness of the integration of body and mind, bringing the riches of body memory and body wisdom. In recollecting this I am freshly inspired by and in awe of this healing work we do.

Bodywise is a book which matters to me very much because it has been a unique opportunity to write about the practices which I most value and which have such a lot to offer to the world: body psychotherapy, ecopsychology, ecodharma and Buddhism. In founding *Somatic Psychotherapy Today* Nancy Eichhorn offers a great gift to those of us working in these fields. *Somatic Psychotherapy Today* is a gift as it is a space in which we can share thoughts and feelings about our practice. We can learn new things and new writers can find their feet in finding their voice, as it were, tackling challenging themes. To me it feels like an experiential, experimental – in the best sense of the word – space which is much needed given that many publications are only accessible to established writers, or those at the top of their tree, or academics. In creating *Somatic Psychotherapy Today* Nancy has cut through those restrictions with a vision to create a publication which is open to all, in the interest of healing.

More than ever we need healing in this crazy world. I know it's not just crazy, it's many things besides, but one can be forgiven for thinking that, tuning into the news in the recent past. Last month the Swiss-born British author Alain de Botton tweeted (2/9/17) that: "Psychotherapy is the single greatest innovation of our times and the discipline on which the eventual flourishing of humankind rests" (Botton, 2017). I'm not sure whether I would personally quite make that claim, but I think it is a point very well made. Psychotherapy, particularly the wholeness of body and somatic approaches, has a lot to offer humankind. It would have even more to offer if it were more accessible, available to more people more of the time, hence the importance of accessible publications and websites like *Somatic Psychotherapy Today*. And to that I would add that ecopsychology and ecodharma - disciplines particularly close to my heart - have a lot to offer other-than-human and more-than-human kind, too, for let's not make the mistake of only paying attention to the flourishing of humankind in this interconnected world.

Bodywise came to life thanks to many, many beings – books are never the product of one person, they are a collective effort, even if one person gets their name on the front cover. In this instance I feel most indebted to therapy clients who come here every week, week in week out, month in, month out, year in, year out. I honour their courage, tenacity, and most of all, their willingness to share their vulnerability and to keep on going, change-making in a world which needs change-makers. I am also very grateful to artist Paul Crummay for painting the front cover after the briefest of descriptions of what I saw in my mind's eye. Finally, and above all, I am indebted to Nancy Eichhorn, midwife of *Somatic Psychotherapy Today* for her vision, perseverance, creativity and great flair for bringing out the best in others and for her love of the world and this work.

Kamalamani
Bristol, England
September 2017

1. Green Tara's Apprentice

In reflecting upon my current work and life the enchanting image of Green Tara comes to mind. Green Tara is a well-known 'bodhisattva' from the Tibetan Buddhist tradition. A bodhisattva is a being who vows to gain enlightenment for the sake of all beings. Tara embodies the altruistic dimension of Buddhist practice and has inspired me since the first retreat I went on in 1995.

What most fascinates me about Green Tara at present is her posture, with one leg up and one leg down. Her left leg is in meditation posture; her right leg is stepping down in compassionate action, serving all beings. She is the embodiment of poised, perfect balance, integrating the polarities of dualistic thinking: inner and outer, self and other, body and mind, being and doing, spirit and matter, male and female, heaven and earth, enlightened and unenlightened. She is said to sit with royal ease in a fully awakened, 'bodhi' state of relaxed yet alert responsiveness:

> The green form of Tara is especially associated with fearlessness and spontaneous helpfulness - like a mother instantly and unthinkingly leaping into danger if her child is threatened, Green Tara steps down at once to give aid and protection to any being who calls on her (Vessantara, 1993: 177).

I find inspiration in contemplating Green Tara's posture, with one leg up in meditation and the other ready to take action. I work as a body psychotherapist, facilitator and writer based in Bristol, England. Green Tara's compassion and balance of her posture are a constant reminder of the balance I need in my work-life. Finding the still point through the integration of being and doing, stillness and action, keeping quiet and making a noise. This works at the subtlest of levels—when do I keep quiet in witnessing the process of a client and when do I intervene, even with the most seemingly gentle and minor of interventions? That balance is an art. Tara makes it look easy . . .

Of course this integration is only possible through a continual expansion of my awareness of body-mind. As I invite the conditions for this process of integration in and with my clients so I echo this process in my own experience and in the quality of my presence and attunement. I say 'continual' which runs the risk of sounding rather linear, chronological, neat and tidy. My experience of embodiment, both personally and as witness, is that it is often more uncertain and unknown than that. Like the elements: earth, water, fire, space, consciousness—our body-minds have their own texture, timing, rhythms and impulses. And what a relief when surrender or a dissolving of stuck energy happens, like a sudden flash of lightening, a spring storm, or a rock fall.

Thinking of my facilitation and training work, what I value most in co-facilitating 'Wild therapy', the form of ecopsychology I teach, is seeing people somehow drop more fully into their experience of being incarnate (human-animal) and part of this interconnected, breathing world. Being in wilder places without a busy schedule and inviting an awareness of the sometimes dance, sometimes tussle, between the wilder and tamer dimensions of ourselves and between one another is simple, profound work supported by the sky above and the solid earth beneath our feet and bums. It is also invaluable work given the times we are living through. The grief work of seeing the harm we have inflicted upon the planet and its species contrasted with the simple, jaw-dropping beauty and awesomeness of nature. The pressing task of staying open and engaged in facing uncertain futures.

We live more closely to the elements during Wild Therapy and in doing so have time and space for a keener awareness and greater intimacy of our own elemental nature. We live more closely with one another in simple conditions, co-creating community and feeling the bonds of our kinship through love and conflict. We witness one other and are witnessed by the other-than-human and more-than-human life around us. Edges soften and hardened fears subside. Living and practising in wilder spots I am reminded of

Tara as forest and wind goddess. The Green form of Tara is particularly associated with the earth, plant life and the wind or air elements. The form of Tara known as Khadiravani often wears lotus flowers in her hair, rather than a jewelled tiara, and lives in a wild pureland (Purna, 1997, 135). Perhaps Khadiravani is the perfect being to represent ecopsychology and ecodharma in her enlightened wildness and reminder of the importance of the breath of life.

I feel gratitude in having 'met' Tara and other Buddha and bodhisattva figures in the course of my Buddhist life and training. I particularly appreciate being introduced to what is known as 'sadhana practice' when I was ordained as a Buddhist. A focal point of sadhana practice is visualising—from the heart—a particular Buddha or bodhisattva figure with which you develop a bond. In a sense sadhana practice is akin to committing to any other long-term relationship (including therapist-client relationships), in that it requires clarity, commitment, mindfulness, and devotion to the process. A useful and unexpected aspect of sadhana is that I have found it useful preparation for entering into depth body psychotherapy work with clients. Cultivating receptivity, being with—without expectations—and taking in as fully as possible the life of another.

It is only now that I realise what a radical and transformative practice sadhana is in a broader societal sense. In our contemporary mainstream culture bodies are viewed with many intentions in mind—fashion-following, lust, envy, pleasure or whatever—but perhaps not so often with the intention of dwelling on the sublime aspects and embodiment (gestures, symbolism, colour) of a particular enlightened quality, be it compassion, wisdom or fearlessness. These qualities resonate with the very same qualities, nascent or well-established, within us.

Dwelling upon the embodiment of the enlightened 'other' feels significant in the current zeitgeist. In a world seemingly obsessed with celebrity culture and reality TV, contemplating enlightening qualities or even beauty in whatever form that takes is, regrettably, less common. On an even simpler level there is something precious about visualising the body of another being whilst staying in connection with my own form and felt senses, further dissolving the mind-made splits between my notions of body and mind, self and other, spirit and matter. Body awareness and our embodied knowing have never felt more important with global record levels of social alienation, poverty, depression and disconnection from ourselves, others, and our relationship with the planet; the body of the earth.

Of course this is old news for readers of *Somatic Psychotherapy Today*, and I have no doubt that I am talking to the converted. But I'm saying it again because it's worth saying - and to re-remind myself! Also because techniques to encourage body awareness seem to be on the increase. Well, techniques to fix most things seem to be on the increase and affirmed by the status quo. As body psychotherapy seems to have experienced something of a renaissance and renewal so have techniques for greater body awareness.

Some of these are really good techniques of course, but they're still techniques in a world which is besotted with quick fixes and short CEU (CPDs) courses with clearly defined and expected learning outcomes. Amongst other things I'm thinking of the rise in popularity of 'mindfulness'. On one hand I think it's great that mindfulness is gaining popularity and having positive results. It seems brilliant that a teaching from an ancient Buddhist 'sutra' (which means teaching, and is literally translated as 'thread') from more than two thousand years ago can help individuals to achieve peace of mind in the 21st century. Yet, knowing how easy it is to get the wrong end of the stick in practising the Dharma from my own hard-worn experience, over and over again, I'm left with some unanswered questions. How effective is it to lift one aspect of a practice out of a tradition of interrelated practices; mindfulness is often taught in Buddhist circles hand in hand with loving-kindness and the ethical precepts, for example. Is the mindfulness promoted in 2012 understood in the same way as taught by the Buddha? What will the longer-term consequences of this be? We'll see.

Likewise, I think we need to revisit over and over the importance of approaching our process and that of our clients and like-minded colleagues with the recognition that we are beings integrating body-mind processes in the here and now. Our body isn't a separate object to be done to, nor are we our body or ultimately defined by our body. I think it's hard to hold these thoughts, even play with these thoughts, given the overwhelming tendencies of our cultural conditioning and the dualistic nature of our minds in wanting to label, name, and fix. In the area of embodiment words start to fall short. I like to recall the words of the Zen master Suzuki and his poetic insightfulness in this quote about the body-mind:

> Our body and mind are not two and not one. If you think your body and mind are two, that is wrong; if you think that they are one, that is also wrong. Our body and mind are both two and one (Suzuki, 1970: 25).

We are a body, and we are not our bodies in any ultimate sense. Our body isn't a well-oiled machine but an inherent part of our incarnation right now. When I die I shall leave this skin, these bones, this flesh and these organs in the earth, even this "I". I have no idea when this will be. Perhaps I'll be more wrinkled with thinning skin, perhaps not. Perhaps I have days to go. It can be challenging to rest with these unknowns, given that our bodies are a wonderful, fallible, mirror-like reminder of old age, sickness, and death. We can touch upon the most mysterious questions about consciousness, bringing in questions from fields as seemingly diverse, at first, as Eastern religion and neuroscience.

At the same time the realm of embodiment is simple, when we remember to remember. Over-thinking doesn't tend to help (I say that from experience!) Am I aware of my breath here and now? Am I present to my experience or recollecting last week or jumping ahead to tomorrow? Can I feel my whole body, or am I more akin to a head on a stick swishing my fingers across the laptop keys? Do I have a broad brush of awareness, or am I aligning myself with a particular story or habit in this moment?

> The human body at peace with itself
> Is more precious than the rarest gem.
> Tsongkapa

So I have come full circle in exploring Tara and her symbolism. In rounding off I am reminded afresh of Tara's left leg in meditation posture. I am reminded to take to my meditation cushion. I meditate because I want to see and relate to myself, others and the world with kinder, wiser, more honest eyes. Sitting helps me to digest and assimilate and provides the space for knowing my own body-mind and dwelling with qualities of the enlightened body-mind in the form of Tara and her friends. In the words of the great 14th century sage, Tsongkapa, I want to be a human body at peace with itself and with the world.

References:
Purna. (1997). 'Tara - Her Origins and Development'. *The Western Buddhist Review*, Vol 2, pp 125-141. Windhorse Publications, Cambridge, UK.
Suzuki, S. (1970). *Zen Mind, Beginner's Mind*. Weatherhill, New York, USA.
Tsongkapa – see below.
Vessantara. (1994). *Meeting the Buddhas: A Guide to Buddhas, Bodhisattvas and Tantric Deities*. Windhorse Publications, Cambridge, UK.

Verse Note:
The full Tsongkapa verse is as follows:
This body of leisure's more valuable than a jewel that gives any wish,
And now is the only time you will ever find a one like this.
It's hard to find, and easily dies, like lightening in the sky.

Think this over carefully, and come to realize
That every action of the world is like the chaff of grain,
And so you must strive night and day to make the most of life.
I, the master meditator, put this into practice;
You, who seek for freedom, must conduct yourselves this way.

This verse is from the very brief version of Lord Tsongkapa's
'Steps on the Path of Buddhahood' which can be found in
Tsongkapa: The Principal Teachings of Buddhism by J.E.
Tsongkapa (author) Geshe Lobsang Tharchin and Michael Roach
(Translators) published in 2004 by Paljor Publications.

2. Wild Horses and Olympic Dreaming

Watching the televised Olympic equestrian events at Greenwich Park in London this summer re-ignited an awareness of my connection with and lifelong love of horses. Seeing the bodies of those fine thoroughbreds coursing and skidding over the cross-country jumps and moving elegantly around the dressage ring re-awoke my early love of the potentially magical, unspoken relationship between horse and human.

Since then I have been paying more attention to horses again, befriending a pair of horses living near a campsite where we were staying on holiday recently and walking the course at a cross-country event not long afterwards. At the event I re-visited my huge admiration for the awesome skills and talents of three-day event riders like Lucinda Green, then Lucinda Prior-Palmer, one of my childhood heroines, and Mark Todd from New Zealand. I was thrilled to see tonnes of exuberant horse galloping past, launching over beautifully-crafted jumps of all shapes and sizes. I remembered one of my ambitions as a 10 year old to win the Badminton Horse Trials in Gloucestershire. Aside from the familiar thrill, a wave of something else rippled through me. At first I couldn't give it a name.

It became clear that it was the bubbling up of sadness. Sadness and an acknowledgement of the central importance of horses and other animals in my life and learning. Waking with the tears of this sadness I realized that the most important things I've learned about trauma and human-inflicted hurt and its after effects I learned through my childhood relationships with horses. It's taken more than three decades to realize that. I never had a horse of my own but was fortunate to look after and occasionally ride friends' horses, to have weekly riding lessons for quite a while, and to go on a memorable – not for all the right reasons - riding holiday in my early teens.

Reflecting more I noted that as a young girl I often ended up being paired with the ponies that needed gentle handling and careful attention. My first experience of this was in the shape of 'Tammy', a lovely, shy, sensitive bay gelding living at the riding stables where I had lessons. Tammy was written off as flighty and a bit mad. But she wasn't, she just became flighty and a bit mad when young hands pulled too hard on her reins, not yet having mastered the art of light contact with the bit in her mouth. So she bolted around the ring at high speed, in an effort, I imagine, to take her place at the back of the line of her horse friends to escape further pulling and jabbing at her mouth. Jumping was even more fun, clinging on as she galloped straight over or through the jumps, colourful wooden poles flying in all directions.

Somehow I always ended up riding Tammy, and we became friends. The trick was to let her have her head. One day I knotted the reigns and let her have her head completely. That was exhilarating as she broke into her habitually fast, skittish canter, and I clung onto the pommel at the front of the saddle. She suddenly realized that no one was pulling at her mouth and relaxed into a softer, more rounded, even stride. From then onwards riding her was a different story. She still flew like the wind but not through fear of being hurt and continually pulled at the mouth.

Another four-legged friend was 'Ladybird', a horse I was lucky enough to have on loan for the best part of a year. Well, kind of lucky. I remember, vividly, the look on my late father's face on her first day at home. We had to resort to calmly cornering her in our neighbor's field with the help of my brother and some bamboo canes as she resolutely refused to be caught. As I approached her, she galloped towards me menacingly and skidded to a halt with feet to spare before rearing up on her hind legs. I persevered and tried to see the world through her eyes of deeply distrusting her two-legged enemies. We slowly, slowly became friends, and I learnt better ways to make contact with her. Eventually she trusted me enough to lift up her legs to pick out her hooves without biting me and brush her rump without kicking me. Towards the end of our time together she trotted towards me, whinnying, like an old friend. She never curbed her habit of jogging sideways up the road. We just learned to avoid main roads . . .

Then there was the tragic memory of a horse friend whose spirit was broken by the rage of his young owner. A scenario where the potentially magical bond and intimacy between horse and human went horribly wrong. It's something I hope never to witness again, the young girl breaking her pony's spirit as her spirit was shattered by the disintegrating of her family's life. So horses have been great friends and teachers to me. In fact, they were my best friends as a girl, along with my German Shepherd dog.

I've found myself wondering what it is that I learnt about trauma and hurt from horses, which I have found so valuable in my work with human beings, especially the clients in my therapy room? Well, I learnt that in no uncertain terms the various behaviours resulted from horses' fear of humans: being thrown off; bolted with (once along a road, ending in serious concussion-not so good); kicked; and gently coaxing a horse out of a state of freeze. The most important thing I learnt, on reflection, was the importance of being in touch with my own thoughts, feelings and embodied sensations and picking up clues—visually, tonally, and kinesthetically—about the horse before approaching him or her.

Communicating with horses feels to me like learning any new language or culture; you need to listen with all your senses, as you do when you're listening to the intonations, pitch and pronunciation of the language you are learning, as well as watching the shape of the lips, as you try to understand the cultural influences which are subtly but significantly different to your own. Most importantly, I've always had a deep respect for horses. I was most struck by that when I encountered the work of the tremendous US horse trainer Monty Roberts and witnessed his deep respect of and love for horses. Perhaps 'talking horse' came relatively easily to me, given my childhood preference for the animal over the human world, and my curiosity and love of both the mystery and ordinariness of connecting. And sometimes I just learnt the hard way and landed in the mud, getting winded and bruised. Horse-riding can be the greatest leveller—quite literally.

I've been curious in recent years by the merging field of 'equine-assisted' psychotherapy, with its focus upon promoting wellbeing for humans through interaction with horses. I've noticed my mixed response to this surge of interest. My most immediate response, given my childhood love of all things equine, is "well, yes of course, that's obviously going to be beneficial". I have also noticed a hint of cynicism in my grown-up (!) view as a therapist. Not cynicism that equine-assisted work wouldn't be valuable, but a fear that it might become another way in which we might exploit our relationship with the animal and other-than-human world. And perhaps, in all honesty, a touch of envy that I don't have a horse and a paddock as a way of offering this work and my lack of growing up with moneyed, pony-clubbing parents. But hey, never say never . . .

I have some qualms about the 'equine-assisted' bit of this work, not dissimilar to some of the concerns I've had about the use of horses in sport, particularly when once-famous race horses are neglected once they are no longer trophy-winners... I know therapy approaches need a name in order to identify them, but I object to the sound of the one-way flow–the horse assists the person. What does the person do for the horse? Are we again using animal and other-than-human life for our own ends? I don't know. I need to mull more on this, for I know first-hand the benefit of equine friendship. Amongst friends who offer equine-assisted therapy, I also witness their deep love and care for their herd. . .

What I also sense, underneath, is a great sadness that we live in the way we do. For many of us, an urban or suburban existence is our everyday reality. We don't get to hang out with horses and other animals. Let's face it, we don't even spend that much time hanging out with friends of our own species! We often don't know the phase of the moon or which crops are ripening or even what sort of soil we might find if we dug down into the earth under our feet. I feel sad most days about how far removed we have become from our wilder habitat, separated by layers of concrete, and our steel boxes as we travel around in cars. We've become more distant from our wilder selves, too. How have we become separated from other life forms, including four-legged equines, to the point where as humans we naturally assume—to our peril–that we are masters and mistresses of the universe?

So today I bow down afresh to the horse. The horses I've been blessed to know and all that they have taught me. I hope I offered them friendship. On a more universal level I'm reminded of how often the horse seems to symbolize strength and freedom. At best, this strength has been admired by different peoples across the world, at worst, man has felt the need to tame and domesticate this strength and wildness in order to suit his own ends. I personally feel deeply appreciative that my connection with the horse is rekindled.

> "If I paint a wild horse, you might not see the horse . . . but surely you will see the wildness!" Pablo Picasso.

Note:
For more information about Monty Robert's work, please visit: http://www.montyroberts.com

3. Touched by the Past in the Present

> Our history is encoded in our body just as the rings of a tree encode the life story of that tree, including its genetic inheritance and the atmospheric conditions that were present from year to year (Stromsted in Johnson & Grand, 1998: 157).

War and peace are on my mind. In particular, the effects of war and peace on our embodiment and our intergenerational connections. We have not long returned from Norway, paying respects to my grandfather who is buried there. I wanted to visit to touch the earth and breathe the air at the final resting place of his remains. He was an airman in Bomber Command in the Pathfinder division of the UK's Royal Air Force, killed towards the end of the Second World War. He and his friends were shot down whilst bombing a u-boat base on the Oslo fjord. He's been dead for 68 years, yet his missing presence has loomed large in the life of my family. Like a heavy cloud with no rain.

Since making this voyage, the clouds have parted. I am changed by the experiences of being in Norway - an earth-touching experience indeed - and I am reminded afresh of the extreme futility of war. Meditating early this evening I find that feelings of loving kindness flow spontaneously for the German soldiers who shot down the plane of my grandfather. Crouching in walled defences as they man their guns. May they be well and happy. They are focused and shouting instructions to one another urgently, breathlessly, in German. May they have survived and lived long and happy lives. They shoot the plane, which starts its long, slow, spiralling, fiery descent to earth. The soldiers are jubilant, congratulating one another momentarily before regaining concentration. May they be alive now, in peaceful retirement. The 'plane explodes in a ball of fire.

My grandfather had a 'safe' job in Bristol; he worked in what was known here as a 'reserved occupation', so consequently wasn't sent to war. My grandfather's father-in-law, my great-grandfather, was killed by a stray bullet whilst he was out for an afternoon stroll in north Bristol. A freak moment in the first day raid of the Battle of Britain in Bristol and the bombing of the Bristol Aeroplane Company. Upset by and indignant about his father-in-law's death, my grandfather joined up and left his safe job behind.

I picture him hunched in his turret as a rear gunner. I dare not see what he saw or feel the fear he felt. I dare not know the suffering he caused. By all accounts a quiet and sensitive man in temperament (bar the odd bout of indignation) I am ashamed to admit that I am relieved he never came home. How could eyes that witnessed the blanket bombing of Dresden and hands that helped to create that towering inferno ever rest easy at night?

Operations reports written by his pilot on the first night of the Dresden bombing say it all: "after the first five minutes he (the controller) said bombing was getting a bit wild...and ordered no more flares". How would a sensitive-hearted man have returned to everyday life, way before the support given nowadays to those suffering from post-traumatic stress disorder? I remember my Nana, my grandfather's wife, with love and a great fondness. How she remembered her lost love. I remember how her slightly brittle exterior was softened by the presence of children, animals, and the mention of her lost love. Her eyes then twinkled like a young girl again, perhaps from an age of greater innocence and ease. As I leave the cemetery in Tonsberg in Norway I feel the eruption of her grief and loss in my heart. Grief which has been frozen reaches boiling point in a matter of shocking seconds.

I imagine how it would be to lose my own love, in the present day. I sense the ghastly shock in reading the words 'missing, presumed dead' and 'killed in action' scribbled hastily in grey pencil on rough cream paper. Words urgent to communicate themselves housed in a scruffy little envelope which has journeyed furiously from the east to the west coast of England. I picture those words, and feel the waiting, longing, and hope shattering to despair, echoing a thousand-fold in the suffering of friends, family, neighbors all around: nearly everyone losing somebody. I sense the moment when the truth reveals itself: he's dead, he's gone, he's not coming home.

A line from Rupert Brooke's poem 'The Soldier' edges its way into my consciousness and suddenly makes perfect sense: 'there's some corner of a foreign field that is forever England' (Brooke, 2010). This cemetery in this small Norwegian town is one of those corners. I realise I have made the trip that my Nana could never make. My body tells me that a task is somehow complete.

I feel huge gratitude. To Jan, the kindly Norwegian who told me the story of his war. How he climbed onto the roof of his house with his friends to wave at the 'armada' of aeroplanes that night, journeying up the Oslo fjord: 73 Lancaster bombers and 12 Mosquito planes. How the town of Horten, his hometown, home of the u-boat base, was lit up by the pathfinder bombers - my grandfather's 'plane amongst those - which made the city "like daylight" in Jan's words. The excitement of war through a child's eyes.

To the Norwegian journalist, his name unknown, who took the secret photos of the airmens' burial and crash site. The photographer was determined to send photos to the relatives of the airmen, to show that they had had a proper ending and to share the story of the end of their lives. His courage in risking his life in capturing those secret images, camera tucked under his winter coat on that snowy March day. To Pastor Knutzen who buried the airmen, insisting they had prayers in their own language, and years later offering friendship to my Dad in the midst of his grief.

I am grateful to friends from Germany. How I can now hear their voices and feel their presence without feeling childhood fear. Fear bred from frozen grief and archaic war films and myths about war heroes, winners and losers, and, in Pablo Neruda's words from his poem 'Keeping Quiet': 'victories without survivors' (Neruda, 1999). Since feeling the eruption of grief and loss in my heart - is this my grief? My loss? My Nana's grief? My father's? Or am I tapping into the universally experience of loss? Most likely all of the above - I have been aware of a thawing process within. I realise that I thought Tonsberg would be a place frozen in time. Time stopped on that icy, moon-lit February night in 1945. What a relief to walk along the waterfront, laugh with locals, wander about and see that Tonsberg is alive and well and that it's the year 2012.

My heart has been softened and strengthened by my funereal, liberating trip up the Oslo fjord. I feel more alive and strangely more relaxed than I've allowed myself to feel. I've fallen a little bit more in love with life, despites its design faults, or perhaps my human design faults. I feel more acutely the times when my heart clamps shut. Why does that heart-closing hurt so much, I ask myself with a new voice, puzzled. In those moments when heart-closing happens I realise that *I* am missing, presumed dead.

I am reminded afresh of the importance of inviting our clients to recognise when they are being touched by their ancestral legacy (see Ancelin Schützenberger, 1998). Honoring the "tying up" up of loose ends of work which are ancestors were unable or disinclined to complete as we each continue to weave the tapestry of our own lives, and its interweaving with those around us; friends and foe. Having been so recently touched by the past in this way myself, I am humbled by the power of the human body to heal itself, if we will just listen to its murmuring and prompts ("for heaven's sake, buy that ferry ticket to Norway!") I am aware, too, of the power of transformation that comes in and through the releasing, dissolving, thawing, discharging - or the particular phenomenon associated with that person's letting go of trauma- and how care-full we need to be in holding that release in our work as therapists.

Most of all the words from Naomi Shihab Nye's 'Kindness' poem roam around in my mind (Shihab Nye, 1998):

> . . . Before you know kindness as the deepest thing inside,
> you must know sorrow as the other deepest thing.
> You must wake up with sorrow.
> You must speak to it till your voice

catches the thread of all sorrows
and you see the size of the cloth...

May all beings be well. May all beings be happy. May all beings be free of suffering.

References:
Ancelin Schützenberger, A. (1998) *The Ancestor Syndrome: Transgenerational Psychotherapy and the Hidden Links in the Family Tree*. Routledge, East Sussex, UK.
Brooke, R (2010) *The Collected Poems of Rupert Brooke*. Forgotten Books. Pp 115.
Neruda, P (1999) *Full Woman, Fleshly Apple, Hot Moon: Selected Poems of Pablo Neruda*. Harper Collins.
Shihab Nye, N. (1998) *Words Under the Words: Selected Poems*. Eighth Mountain Press

4. Mammal Body

Our bodies are wild. The involuntary quick turn of the head at a shout, the vertigo of looking off a precipice, the heart-in-the-throat in a moment of danger, the catch of the breath, the quiet moments relaxing, staring, reflecting—all universal responses of the mammal body . . . The body does not require the intercession of some conscious intellect to make it breathe, to keep the heart beating. It is to a great extent self-regulating, it is a life of its own (Snyder, 1990: 17).

I've been watering the plants in my therapy room. It is rapidly becoming like a jungle. At least a little jungle in the suburbs. There is a fig, spider plant, butterfly palm, calathea, hypoestes, peace lily, bromeliad, Boston fern, yucca, and a few mystery guests of unknown species. Nearly all of the plants have been adopted from others: my Mum, and nearby neighbors who have left them out in the street, a little limp and sad-looking ready for the rubbish collection.

This room is like no other room in our house. It is quite plain, with the main feature being the plants. I love the fact that there are far more plant beings than human beings in this room. I love their different colours, heights, and textures. I love the shadows of the plants cast at night by the floor-level lights. I have enjoyed and have sometimes been confused by the process of figuring out what it is that makes each of them thrive and flourish, paralleling work with clients and supervisees.

What I have most appreciated in the time I've been working in this beautiful, simple room, a little over two and a half years, is that which I've learnt about nurturing and care, in particular, returning to a state of nurturing and care when things don't go to plan, which, of course, they often don't. In fact, I plan far less in my own life the older I get. Of course, I've learnt about nurturing and care through my continuing and deepening work with clients, supervisees and trainees in this room. But this morning I've been realising what I've learnt about nurturing and care of myself and my own self-regulation at the beginning of the middle years of my life.

This morning, the plants in my therapy room were powerful symbols of the capacity to attend to the other: human and other-than-human and more-than-human. In the case of the plants: feeling the dryness of the soil, removing dead leaves, misting, feeding, tweaking – "are you happy there, fern?" A month ago my partner and I became tenants of a local allotment (community garden) just three minutes' walk from home. This feels like part of the same process of attending to other and in doing so, also attending to self. For the past two years we've been on the waiting list for an allotment and for nearly two years before that I was trying to convince my partner he actually wanted one (thankfully he came round to the idea). I have fallen in love with a little patch of neglected earth. Grubbing around in the soil, sowing seeds in pots, pruning in driving rain and thunder and lightning, and shaping beds have been the highlights of my month. I'm surprised to find that I particularly appreciate the fact that we don't own this land; we are its stewards.

This field has its unique history. Since enclosure, it has been part of a local farm and more recently the field upon which the local funeral director kept the black horses which used to pull the carts carrying coffins before the times of motorised hearses. I love this equine link (think two editions ago and my singing the praises of 'Wild horses and Olympic dreaming'). Historically these fields have also been used as gardens, orchards and for the site of Sunday-school outings and picnics. The fields overlook East Bristol where some of my paternal ancestors were long-standing market gardeners. For much of the 20th century and now in the 21st century these fields have been carved lovingly into allotments and rented to local people to grow their fruit, veggies and, nowadays, flowers, too.

It is a lovely part of Bristol. For years I have been walking along the medieval lane along the top of the allotments en route to the local common. The allotment lane runs along a high ridge of land running north-east, with views of the suburbs of south-east Bristol, stretching all the way to a line of hills which acts as a natural barrier between Bristol and the neighbouring city of Bath. At one of the highest point sits Kelston Round Hill, a hill we overlook from our bedroom window. On a morning of low mist and rising sunlight it has something of the enchantment of a distant Vale of Avalon.

It has been fascinating to get to know 'our' patch of land. Fascinating and, at times, a little disquieting. The land has been neglected. At times this has reminded me tangibly of neglect I have experienced in my own body and those of my clients. When we were first being shown the three plots on offer ours was by far the most overgrown, dominated by a central patch of wild, overgrown fruit bushes, an apple tree, and a large stagnant pond at the bottom of the land. Given how busy each of us are, this was by far the most demanding and least sensible allotment to take on, and yet, well it just kind of chose us. I looked across at my partner, praying he wouldn't plump for the more realistic not so very overgrown option. He looked at me, smiled, and nodded knowingly, and the decision was made.

There's been lots to do. My surprise is that this doing has been the most therapeutic, practical, hard work I've ever done. It's been a difficult midwinter and early spring. A close friend and work colleague in my family business died suddenly in her sleep before Christmas. She and I shared an office for many years and were intimate in the way workmates become intimate: sharing the bits of life that seem so mundane but pattern our everydays. I have been bewildered by shock and grief and a temporarily doubled workload, with echoes of my Dad dying on the job nine years previously.

My partner and I have taken on the allotment during the phase of the subsiding of shock and disbelief and the emergence of softer, moister grief. As often happens with grief, my body reminds me of earlier grief and losses, and in parallel, an acknowledgement of where I am and how I am now. What life looks like, what I'm doing with the time available to me, and how I deal with the fact that none of us know how long that time will be. Will I be three score years and 10, three years older than my dear Dad at his death, or 45, like my workmate?

Clearing, weeding, shovelling, pruning and planting have plonked that question into perspective in no uncertain terms. The allotment has got me outside in all weathers, in the thick of the elements, calling me to work. It's been the coldest March since 1962 in England – there has been a lot of weather, internal and external! Working the allotment has been hugely cleansing and reparative. My life has been patterned by a fair amount of grief and loss, as well as losses that have shaped my close loved ones. In terms of my own self-regulation I can revert easily to early strategies and 'brittling up' and pushing through grief. I watch myself withdraw in dread and silent terror, resonating right back to early terrors. This winter I have more often than not been quiet rather than withdrawn and find I am becoming re-acquainted with neglected parts of myself. That re-acquaintance has taken place in surprising ways, with myself, trusted others and this patch of land.

In living this bit of life I have re-experienced something of my 'mammal body' to which Gary Snyder (1990) refers in the opening quote: "The involuntary quick turn of the head at a shout, the vertigo of looking off a precipice, the heart-in-the-throat in a moment of danger, the catch of the breath, the quiet moments relaxing, staring, reflecting". The tsunami of shock through my body this winter has caught me unawares. And I've come back to earth through working with and relating to this little patch of land, with its own life, history, beauty, neglect and plant knowledge, for don't forget, plants know things too! (Chamovitz, 2012). No wonder, then, that horticultural therapy and ecopsychological practices are increasingly popular.

We have both wanted to follow quite intuitively what we find on this patch of land. We've pruned hard in what we lovingly call the 'fruit forest': clearing and pruning so that the swamped apple tree avoids being completely choked to death by the tangle of both its own earth-burrowing branches and the wild growth of its gooseberry, redcurrant, and blackcurrant neighbors. But we've also wanted to follow the natural shapes that we find. So the top bed is egg-shaped, apt, because we worked on it on Easter Sunday with the goddess Oestra in mind. It follows the curve of the path on one side and the curve of the autumn raspberries on the other.

It will take years to learn what does and doesn't grow here, which other beings live and feed from this earth. Then there's been re-acquaintance on a community level. I've lived in this neighborhood for many years but I've had more conversations with fellow allotment holders, also neighbors, than I've ever had in such a short time period. I've put names to faces to whom I've been saying good morning for years. I am struck by generosity: "borrow my fork", "have these spare onion sets", and the curiosity in seeing just how differently people approach their relationship with their patches of land, how different yet how similar we humans are in our weird and wonderful styles and strategies in living.

Something goes on in these ". . . quiet moments relaxing, staring, reflecting" between raking and weeding. We slow down, we get our hands dirty, we hear the birds, and perhaps we have more time for ourselves and one another.

> The ground that is cultivated in the garden is common ground, shared by many and host to multitudes. Every particle of soil, every atom of earth, is alive with mystery and potential all stirred up together. Every soil is a long winding story, told in the voices of water and inhaled and exhaled air, of the stone-slow cycle of rock itself becoming soil, and in the voices of the swarming masses of microorganisms feeding, breathing and dying on fertile dust, creating new life out of their bodies made from exploded stone (Johnson, 2008: 88).

References:
Chamovitz, D. (2012). *What a Plant Knows: A Field Guide to the Senses of Your Garden and Beyond.* Oneworld Publications.
Johnson, W. (2008). *Gardening at the Dragon's Gate: at Work in the Wild and Cultivated world.* Bantam Trade Paperbacks.
Snyder, G. (1990). *The Practice of the Wild.* Counterpoint.

Bibliography:
Gerhart, S. (2004). *Why Love Matters: How Affection Shapes a Baby's Brain.* Routledge
Orbach, S. & Carroll, R (2006). 'Contemporary Approaches to the Body in Psychotherapy: Two Psychotherapists in Dialogue' in Corrigall et al (eds) (2006) *About a body: Working with the Embodied Mind in Psychotherapy.* Routledge.
Stauffer, K. (2009). 'The Use of Neuroscience in Body Psychotherapy: Theoretical and Clinically Relevant Aspects', in Hartley, L. (Ed.). (2008). *Contemporary Body Psychotherapy: the Chiron Approach.* Routledge.
Totton, N. (2003). *Body Psychotherapy.* Open University Press.

5. Holding to Nothing Whatever

> Freedom means nonattachment, which is not indifference but rather the penetration of absolute truth. To see that clearly, we let go for one moment of anything that we call our own, anything that we like or consider important. We examine it until its fleeting nature has become quite apparent (Khema, 1999: 117-118).

I find myself free associating as I bring to mind attachment, the theme of this autumn edition of *Somatic Psychotherapy Today*. Attachment as discussed in Bowlby's classic studies, attachment in terms of the teachings of going beyond ego-clinging from Buddhist teachings, as well as the free-flowing images and reflections floating readily to the surface of my consciousness.

At the Zoo
The image of my nephew, aged three, during a visit he and I make to Bristol Zoo one warm summer's day. He dashes towards the marine tank, pointing excitedly at the penguins; lost in a watery world, his little frame swamped by the huge aquamarine tanks full of excited life. Moments later a flash of anxiety, and he scours the crowd to find me. He runs back to my side and grabs my hand. A few minutes later he looks up at me, looks across at the monkey cage, looks at me again and decides to go it alone once more, trying out his new-found toddling independence. After meeting the monkeys he dashes back to the safety of my hand-hold. I feel like a living example of one of Bowlby's research subjects.

Remembering Ruby
I am at a fundraising event organised by one of my workmates. He continues to do an amazing job of raising money for the charity Meningitis UK, supporting them to find a vaccine for this scarily swiftly-acting disease. As he runs the raffle there is a fleeting moment when he falters. It's so fleeting that to most people it goes unnoticed. Inside the body of this tall, upright, courageous man is a mending broken heart. He mourns the sudden death of his daughter, Ruby. Ruby by name and by nature; embodying her jewel name, she was a sparkling and fun-loving little girl. He and Ruby's attachment defies death and her memory lives in his heart and in his enduring efforts to help other bereft families.

Bonds of Friendship
We celebrate the 70th birthday of a very old friend and neighbour with her daughters and friends. Years pass and we don't see each other and yet those enduring bonds are just there. Bonds forged in baby paddling pools, charging around on ponies, and rainy days playing together at home. These bonds are a poignant reminder of connection at a time when I find myself at cross-purposes with another friend. We are in dispute. We are in one of those scenarios when the differences in our characters, our opposite-ends-of-a-telescope perceptions, and our diverging life plans mean that it feels impossible to find ground where we can meet. It's not yet the time for reconciliation; it's a no-man's-land – no woman's land - time of patiently attending and limiting judgments.

Client Endings
Therapy-wise I feel twinges of sadness following the ending of two long-term clients this summer. Last Friday one flew home to the States. His leaving the country somehow amplified this ending compared to other endings. I wonder: Did he get his flight okay? How was his homecoming? How will the transition from UK to US life be? My maternal counter-transference continues, and I feel the tangible loss of the privilege which it is to work with someone

intimately over many years; the same time each week, season by season, year in, year out.

Reflections

I am most interested in attachment not as a theory, not simply the contents of a text book, but as a process we're all in, we're all doing, or perhaps avoiding doing, all of the time. Of course we have our powerful pre and peri-natal and childhood imprints of our notions of attachment or lack thereof. We are born seeking contact for our own survival, nourishment, our sense of ourselves and our relational, gendered place in the world. In terms of the work of Wilhelm Reich and character structure, we seek to attach or detach in character (Reich, 1990). We do our best figuring out the big questions of how to be, how to feed, how to assert our independence - with our toddling little legs - how to trust our body's cycles and our sense of autonomy, trying out our thrusting power and taking on our sexual, gendered identity in the big, wide world.

The subject of how we approach contact with others, seeking to consciously and unconsciously make and sometimes break attachments with others, in character, is a subject close to my heart. It is the theme of my first book *Meditating with Character* (Kamalamani, 2012). The book's contents weave together post-Reichian character structure with meditation and reflection exercises, resting on the Buddhist teaching of the 'three laksanas'. The three laksanas teach of the unsatisfactoriness, impermanence and insubstantiality of life. How we come unstuck when we relate to life as if it were constantly satisfying, never changing and consisting of people, places and events that are fixed rather than also in constant flux. How we find wide-winged freedom through loosening our self and world views, our attachment to certain outcomes and circumstances, and realising the creative facets of our character conditioning.

Our ego-clinging to a view of ourselves and others as satisfying, constant and fixed in nature causes us suffering. In our 'me-making' we forget to remember that we aren't the center of the universe after all. "Shock horror, she doesn't agree with me!" Or "He sees the world differently! (How dare he!)" The antidote to attachment is to dwell upon the reality of the nature of how things are, how our lives unfold in front of us: happy, sad, neutral, often in the course of just one morning, ever-changing and flowing, rather than reliable and samey.

This teaching sounds so simple, is so simple, but is trickier to practise. I have seen myself and others create problems for ourselves in taking the teachings on ego-clinging to mean flatly denying our human attachment to others. Ouch. It can be easy to fall into the trap of thinking of enlightenment as a rather detached, cool state of being - even an escape. Meditating far from the world. Removed from, or beyond the tangles, confusions, and delights of everyday life. That's not my perception of enlightenment. Enlightening moments witness our connection with all that lives; human and other-than-human, imbued with compassionate and wise action.

And Buddhas have characters too! When we've fully awoken and dusted ourselves off to reveal Buddha nature, some of us will tend to be more reserved and detached, others more full-blooded and passionate. All the while we practise the art of muddling through the lotus pond of life. It's helpful to remove ourselves from the conditions of our everyday life from time to time, not as an escape but as an experiment in seeing what happens to our hearts, minds and actions in a different context. But, of course, we have our enlightening moments here, in this body, in the midst of this precious human life wherever we're standing or sitting or walking.

Our human bodies want to, need to attach, in terms of sensing contact with ourselves and other beings. It's the most human thing to want to make contact. In fact, it's survival. It is the nature of this attachment that can tangle us up; when we start expecting the other to see the world through our eyes; when we treat each context as if it were our family of origin; or when we struggle to understand the other's world view, making them wrong rather than clocking the vast differences between us.

Just as our amazing, beautiful bodies are subject to old age, sickness and death - not as permanent as we would sometimes like - so our attachments with others are unpredictable: the Mum who isn't ready for motherhood and hasn't the capacity to nurture her child; the client who disappears; the father whose own wilfulness is threatened by his toddler's temper tantrums; the child who dies; the lover who leaves, finding love elsewhere; or the long-term friend with whom we find ourselves parting company.

Attaching, detaching, living and loving, it is a never-ending Herculean task. How do we live and love fully, attaching and detaching, knowing in our bones the truth of impermanence and insubstantiality? Is it possible? How do we build rapport with clients? Friends? Family? Do we show only our professional persona to clients, or allow our own character to permeate beautifully and authentically our therapeutic presence and responses? Is it easier to hide in a monastery with our monkey-like mind to tame? Or easier to rocket full-throttle into everyday life with all its 'honey on a razor's edge' distraction?

I guess we start from where we are, with honest eyes, heart, and guts, which expand to compassion for ourselves and others. Even with 'good enough' parents or carers we have our own work to do in understanding our own quirks and strengths in relating to ourselves and others, whether we're six or 66.

In understanding my own attachments and character I find myself simultaneously accepting who I am, and, in parallel, never accepting who I am in the sense of fixing myself, boxing myself in and turning from freedom. In the meantime I cultivate cajoling compassion for the bits of my experience and history with which I continue to struggle. Our relationship with our attachment patterns and character are, too, in constant flux. Moving through the different cycles of life: babyhood, childhood, teens, middle years, eldership, and surfing the unpredictability of life's circumstances, we are brilliant work in progress.

In amongst the flux I am reminded of a line from the 'Heart Sutra', one of the most popular and quoted Buddhist scriptures:

Holding to nothing whatever,
But dwelling in Prajna wisdom
(FWBO, 1999).

References:
Kamalamani. (2012) *Meditating with Character,* Mantra Books, an imprint of John Hunt Publishing, Hampshire, UK.
Khema, A. (1999) *Be an Island: The Buddhist Practice of Inner Peace*. Wisdom Publications, Boston.
FWBO (1999) *Puja: The FWBO book of Buddhist Devotional Texts*. Windhorse Publications. 6th edition. This particular translation of the 'Heart Sutra' is by Philip Kapleau Roshi.
Reich, W. (1990) *Character Analysis*. Third edition. Farrar, Straus and Giroux (FSG), New York, USA.

6. Diagnosing

This winter edition of *Somatic Psychotherapy Today* has got me digging deep in looking at diagnosis: how I understand the term, how I read the body and what I do in the place of diagnosis, at least in terms of the more normative and medicalized usage of the term. I am glad that medics are experts in diagnosis, but for me it's not a term that makes much sense in my work. When I was in training as an integrative counselor I first heard the words 'diagnosis' and 'treatment plan' being used with reference to clients. I was taken aback at the strength of my response, wanting nothing to do with this way of conceiving of people. It didn't resonate with me then and it still doesn't.

Curiously, in the years that have passed, a significant proportion of clients who have come to me have come with the expressed wish of wanting to escape the medical model, to go beyond the label of their former diagnosis. I am struck by their often complex relationship with their diagnostic label. On the one hand it seems to give comfort in its familiarity, somehow giving the individual a pigeon-holed identity and, in parallel, something of a ball and chain in terms of their freedom to be who they are in the present day, having 'recovered'.

My clients aren't here to be fixed, but they certainly want to change - including changing the bits that don't want to change, even though that's the hardest work. My job is to work attentively in a relational and embodied way; gathering information about them and their patterns, noticing and working with symptoms and embodied metaphors in terms of understanding the creativity and constraints of their particular character and context.

In mulling the whole area of diagnosis the universe helped out in a timely way. Whilst I was watching a historical television documentary, I was reminded by the narrator of the origins of the word 'diagnosis'. The original Greek definition of diagnosis relates, in part, to the word 'gnosis' and the understanding of spiritual mysteries. This was a relief. I could definitely overcome my reactivity and write 1,500 words about knowing deeply my clients and their preferred patterns and strategies, knowing the evolving shape of our therapeutic relationship and having a keen interest in spiritual mysteries! The way I think about my clients before, during, and post my work with them seems to me more akin to being a psycho-spiritual detective than a health worker with a drug cabinet.

The therapeutic process begins well before the client walks into my therapy room. Do they phone, email or stop me having heard me give a public talk? Or perhaps they've been given my name by a friend. Do they phone simply to hear my voice and feel assured that my website has given them all the information they need? Do they email, attempting to avoid voice contact at all costs, until meeting in person?

Is their contact casual or urgent? Specific or vague? Ingratiating or hasty? Do they show up or disappear into the ether, perhaps re-surfacing a year later? Are they eager to pay before we start or do they nearly forget?

This is all, potentially, vital relational information. The way I respond or react is of equal importance, sometimes telling me of differences in habit and etiquette, sometimes hints of possible transferences to come, sometimes that I'm simply feeling grumpy. My task is to note this information carefully, whilst holding it lightly, doing my best to meet the person in front of me as fully as possible, without preconceived pictures, ideas and assumptions.

I notice as clients enter the hallway, make first contact, take off their shoes, climb the stairs, find the right door, and notice what – if anything – they notice about the room, negotiate which chair to sit in, how they hold themselves and breathe once they are seated. I'm noticing their shape: physical and energetic, the flow or staccato-nature of their walk, their pace. I notice what's happening with my felt senses and movements. I try and watch without watching, not wanting to be invasive even on a subtle level, given that I attract sensitive souls and know how I feel if I know someone's scrutinizing me too closely without that having been somehow negotiated, albeit in a non-verbal way. I'm not too bad at this, being an inveterate people-watcher, but it calls for sensitivity and kind eyes.

As the client's world unfolds in the initial session – I always see clients for an initial session before we both decide to work together – I watch for what's not being said. What's flickering at the edges of my awareness? If I feel inexplicably distracted, I attend even more fully to what's going on in the room— maybe muffled emotion or distracted energy—and let words wash over me as only one channel of information. I notice how my body wants to be present with this person. Bolt upright, a little slumped, or somewhere between? Or perhaps my feet would rather be pacing the floor? What's today's story of this body? What will constellate around this therapeutic relationship?

And so I begin the process of learning how to make contact with this person and them with me. I get fairly early indications as to whether making contact is going to occupy the whole of the therapeutic process, or whether contact-ful rapport is more likely to come more easily with this particular client. Then I start information-gathering. I've seen how this being arrives, now what are the words that bring them here? What was the trigger? Why now? Why me? I hope not to ask too many questions and generally manage to find out what matters to the client without interfering with their flow.

With diagnosis in mind, I've racked my brain in the past few weeks, asking myself whether I do something akin to diagnosis and devising a plan of treatment. I don't, although I think and reflect upon my work with clients and cherish supervision. Whilst I have a clear sense of the stated concerns of the client - if they've articulated them - these can soon change and a lot of life can happen in the week between therapy sessions. My job, as per two of the definitions of diagnosis from our well-thumbed shorter Oxford English dictionary, is to know distinctly and to know deeply the person in front of me - including their spiritual mysteries... We may contract carefully and review regularly but a vital therapeutic ingredient is keeping space open so the client can inhabit the spontaneous, fresh, and unexpected, whilst being in a safe enough, confidential space where they are free to experiment with different thoughts, ideas, voices, movements, and behaviors.

With some clients I work in a way which is closely informed by post-Reichian character structures, which I find invaluable (see Reich, 1990 and Totton, 2009). I'll sometimes explain character structure to some clients if I think they will find it useful, whilst with others I use it as an aid to my own understanding and in supervision. I find character structure interesting in terms of the debate about the extent to which it's some sort of type theory. I've two dear colleagues, one an existentialist psychotherapist and the other a phenomenological psychotherapist, who have no time for character structure at all, feeling that it pigeon-holes people. We agree to disagree!

Their perception is in contrast to my own experience of working with character, in terms of both my expanding self-awareness and in providing a vital model for working with some clients, some of the time. Character structure can throw light on our engrained patterns, give us some useful insights into our strategies and deepest, blind spot defenses and yet those defenses can change. How liberating...

I also feel indebted to Reich for bringing in the importance of the cultural conditions which shape us profoundly at conception, birth, and in our early, growing years. We are social beings, relational beings, and conditioned beings. We are beings in flux. It's always a useful reminder to me to remember the wider webs of which clients are a part. I am of late saddened to see how an increasing number of clients and supervisees are negatively impacted by economic, political, and ecological problems. Scarcity borne of policies of austerity, loss of income, and fear for our collective future and the world we are leaving our children. The clients sitting in front of us are products of their/our culture. We, as therapists, are also the product of our cultures and subcultures. So as we 'diagnose' or 'read' our clients, in whatever way we personally choose to do that, we are simultaneously taking the temperature of the wider culture.

Reading the body of my client and being as present as possible in my own body is a foundation of practising Embodied-Relational therapy. I'm a therapist and in parallel, I'm a midwife, witness, confident, mentor, teacher, sounding board, and, as the transference develops, provisional mother, father, brother, sister, daughter, son, lover, and fairy God mother and enlightened being (gulp). To know the particularity of someone, and to know them deeply, is a process, rather than a defined treatment plan.

On rainy autumn days when therapy work feels hard I draw upon the inspiration of Amitabha, a Buddha figure with whom I have cultivated a bond through meditation and everyday practice for the past decade. Amitabha, well-known in the Mahayana school of Buddhism, abides in the mythical western quarter and is associated with infinite light and boundless compassion. His particular wisdom, given that each Buddha is associated with a different facet of enlightened wisdom, is that of discriminating wisdom. He sees the particularity and the uniqueness of all things, which puts me in mind of the definition of diagnosis as being distinguishing and discerning. Amitabha cherishes and delights in the uniqueness of each moment, every individual, of a single flower in the grass. His is a wisdom that sees the beauty and uniqueness of everything and every moment, at the same time seeing their unity. May wisdom pervade my therapy work – and yours.

References:
Reich, W. (1990) *Character Analysis*. Third edition. Farrar, Straus and Giroux (FSG), New York, USA.
Totton, N. and Edmondson, E. (2009) *Reichian Growth Work: Melting the Blocks to Life and Love*. Second edition. PCCS Books, Ross-on-Wye, UK.

7. The Body Politic

In May this year I'm co-ordinating a conference: 'The Body Politic'. It is being hosted in London by UK-based Psychotherapists and Counsellors for Social Responsibility (PCSR) as its 7th annual Psychotherapy and Politics conference. I am a steering group member of PCSR and editor of its in-house publication *Transformations*. The idea for this event came to me nearly four years ago, at my first steering group meeting. I envisaged an event exploring creatively, honestly, and constructively what it means to be a body. A body shaped by the social, political, ecological and economic backdrop and dynamics unfolding before and throughout our lives; by our thoughts, feelings, beliefs, patterns, actions, and allegiances; by our connection - or lack, thereof - with the earth and other-than-human and more-than-human life. I hope that the keynotes, workshops, and discussions of this event will not only highlight the struggle to reclaim our bodies as our own, within the complex networks of power which we inhabit, but also to celebrate being a body.

So the theme of 'the body in relationship: self-other-society' is timely and very much on my mind. It's also starting to dawn on me - to my surprise, if I'm honest - how contentious and stirring a theme this may prove to be. A surprise to me because, working as a body psychotherapist, being a meditator and teacher of embodying meditation, and being interested in what's going on in the world around me, I'm concerned everyday with how society has shaped and continues to shape our incarnation, for good and ill. Yet, we don't - in the UK, at least - talk much in depth about these themes. Not even in therapists' circles or body psychotherapy circles. It still feels a bit fringe, despite the manifestations of our politicised bodies in the mainstream in the shape of body dysmorphia, addiction to a range of drugs of choice - some more socially acceptable than others - and self-harm, to name but a few.

And on a much bigger scale, the shadow of our embodiment, or lack of embodiment, is reflected in the way we are treating the planet, and other-than-human species, eroding our home and the home of billions of others.

I don't want to get too doom and gloom here. Being a body brings moments of bliss: being drunkenly orgasmic, feeling the beat of a drum resonating with our body's beat until we don't know which beat is which, losing ourselves in wild dancing, sitting quietly, wholly, and contentedly in meditation, holding our wrinkled-face new-born after a long, arduous labour, and those ordinary magic moments of connection breaking bread and drinking wine with cherished friends and family.

The experience of being a body can, and is, hell on earth for billions of our global neighbours. The United Nations Food and Agriculture Organization estimates that nearly 870 million people of the 7.1 billion people in the world, or one in eight, were suffering from chronic undernourishment in 2010-2012 (1). 30 million women, children, and men are victims of human trafficking, modern-day slavery, every year (2). In Africa alone, 345 million people lack access to water for drinking, washing, and cleaning (3).

Perhaps these seem like extreme examples, taking place in a far continent, and it's just too much to take in these facts. This is a feeling I know intimately, being flooded with overwhelm or falling into horrified anxiety before switching off in order to cope with the challenges and fullness of everyday life. Perhaps it's easier to recall clients closer to home. Those people we've welcomed into our therapy rooms who are struggling with substance abuse, or who are asylum seekers exiled from home, or who are victims of bullying or domestic violence, or who are starving themselves, literally, to death, or who have narrowly escaped losing their life in a war zone. How do our bodies respond to these clients? How do we assimilate and digest hearing the sharing of these experiences? What resonates in our own experience? Which prevailing emotions arise? Fear? Anxiety? Tenderness? Compassion? Most likely a potent mingling mixture.

I am interested in how we create more dialogue about these themes; how we draw upon our wealth of experience from our own history of embodiment and in witnessing this in hundreds of our clients. Perhaps we could speak out a little more? Speaking out, it seems, is not something which many therapists find all that easy. This feels a bit of a shame and lost opportunity given the hundreds of hours each year we spend reflecting on the nature of what it means to be alive and embodied.

This week on the PCSR steering group we've been finalising our flyer for this May 'Body Politic' event. It's been a fascinating process in many ways. And a difficult one. Firstly, it's really really tricky to find images of bodies which aren't airbrushed and made to look beautiful in a very conventional sense. It's not easy finding photos of ordinary folk going about their lives, much easier to find highly sexualised images. Secondly, the more I thought of the theme, the more I was aware that I would miss or fail to represent a group of people whose lives are severely hampered by body politics: those whose bodies don't conform to the majority: physically, sexually, in terms of gender, skin colour, class, ability, and cast, those who are victims of war and torture. We ended up deciding that it was too hard-hitting to include an image of covered corpses who were victims of war in Iraq, for example. Some felt that such an image had no place in our advertising for a UK psychotherapy event. In my mind, it has everything to do with us and UK foreign policy, yet I can see the inherent dangers in further de-sensitising readers, or worst still, leading them to switch off and not come to the conference to engage with the debates.

The politics of being a body are going on all the time in and out of our therapy rooms. The use, misuse, and denial of power and potency, consciously and in the shadows. We/I have our own embodied prejudices, assumptions, excellences, and these inevitably work their way into our therapeutic work, hence the importance of supervision, peer support, awareness of our privileges and life with enough balance. We hopefully know enough about the conditions which have led to the oppression and liberation in our own bodies, and how we work with what that, and how we can, albeit indirectly and unconsciously, fall into contributing to the oppression of others, particularly if we are less familiar with recognising our own privileges. The awareness-raising work we can do leads to greater freedom for ourselves, our clients, and those around us.

As body psychotherapists and body workers, it seems to be critically important that we know our own power and potency and acknowledge the impact we have. Not in a big ego way, but in a responsible being way. We need meaningful rites of passage so we honour our body-minds in whatever stage of life we are dwelling. We need to know that we are creatures living amongst other creatures, neither better nor worse than the other species with whom we share the planet. Perhaps we need to pay a bit more attention to our relationship with our environment and the wider world. Not just so we stay healthy and grounded (though that's useful), but so we can listen more accurately to our bodies and the bodies of others—learning from the rhythms of our bodies and the seasons. Maybe we need to remind ourselves of the actual or potential bliss of being a body, too, remembering we are beings made of flesh, blood, and bones, not consumers as capitalism likes to define us, or rational men as economists like to depict us. No, we're flesh and blood, beautifully messy, simple and complex beings. Maybe in 2014 we can balance who we are on the inside and the outside, although in truth, such a distinction doesn't really exist. Find space to tend to our rich inner world, occupying the space we take up and looking out for our fellow beings near and far, human and other-than-human.

Note:
For information about Psychotherapists and Counsellors for Social Responsibility please visit: http://www.pcsr.org.uk/

Web References:
(1) http://www.worldhunger.org/articles/Learn/world%20hunger%20facts%202002.htm Accessed 14th January 2014.
(2) http://www.notforsalecampaign.org/?gclid=CKHVv_Tf_rsCFQMYwwodrRgAwg Accessed 14th January 2014.

8. Consuming passions

I'm learning how to taste everything.
(Laurie Halse Anderson, 2014: 276).

To lose confidence in one's body is to lose confidence in oneself.
(Simone de Beauvoir, 2010: 355).

    I have puzzled over the psychology of food, body image, sexuality, gendered identity, and being called a girl and a woman since I was little. I grew up with a beautiful mother and grandmother who were absorbed by fashion and being attractive. The language around food consisted of "being good" versus "being naughty". As a girl, I found fashion and food pretty boring; I was a tomboy, roaming the countryside and trotting around on borrowed horses, reading adventure stories, enjoying freedom and wildness. Freshly-groomed horse was my favourite smell, rather than Chanel No. 5. Fashion-conscious wise, body-wise, even, I couldn't help thinking I was a bitter disappointment to my elegant female folk.
    These days I am repeatedly saddened by the self-hatred and self-harming of so many of my female clients, and a few of the male ones, and a few who would sooner not be identified as either female or male. I'm sickened by the suffering of teenage girls and the rising numbers of boys who are starving themselves, some to death, whilst millions of other humans in the world are dying of malnutrition, against a backdrop of rising obesity. The politics of food and confusion around eating, consumption, and nourishment have never been more bewildering in a world full of beings hungry for love and connection.

In writing this article, I find it impossible to talk about the psychology of food without touching on the themes of body image, gender, sexuality, and identity, and notice the old echoes of fear and shame that emerge for me in this territory. I know I'm not alone in this; in fact, I'm in good company. I haven't met many women who grew up with a healthy, balanced attitude to food, eating, and their bodies. I've met a few women who reached womanhood largely unscathed, but sadly they're in a minority.

Since my girlhood, I've been familiar with the latest fad diets. I witnessed my Mum's valiant efforts with the: Mayo diet; the F plan; and the Hip and Thigh diet, to name but a few. I became a child-expert in food-as-the-currency-of-love through daily culinary interactions with my thin grandmother. Woe betides anyone who didn't clear their plates and come back for seconds. Food was not only the currency of love but sadly a powerful bartering tool in the love-hate relationship between my mother and grandmother – and they traded quite ferociously.

Then puberty happened. I realised, with some shock and resistance that my body was changing, and I, too, was expected to join the world of women. I wasn't ready to swap my wellington boots for heels and handbags. So I didn't. But I did realise I was severely ill-prepared for decoding the unspoken assumptions and expectations of what it means to be a woman and how muddled that was in my head: a rich cocktail of food, nourishment, body image, love, and the scary realm of sexuality. My embodied defense was the layer of retained puppy fat between me and the world keeping others, particularly the opposite sex, at bay.

This messy thinking and armored defense was compounded by a routine visit to my local doctor. He confirmed what I already feared in my belly: I was "socially unacceptable" for being a stone and a half overweight. In fact, his full verdict was that: "it's socially unacceptable for a *teenage girl* to be overweight" (my italics). He didn't ask me about eating habits, or exercise, or nutrition. Instead he lectured me about social unacceptability. I failed to check out what his judgment would have been had I been a teenage boy. I wish, in hindsight, he had checked my thyroid's health - he could have eased much suffering then and in the decades to come.

What was also emerging for me at that point was a genuine interest in nutrition and the workings of the body. Studying biology, and later for an exam in nutrition and cookery, I was fascinated by nutrition and health. I also realised that I was a good cook, which remains a creative, relaxing outlet. I was amazed by the workings of the body. I loved the intricate diagram-drawing of biology classes at which I excelled, and have memories of Tuesday afternoon experiments, in particular, boiling a peanut in a test tube to find out its calorific value. Not long afterwards, I decided to become vegetarian and became increasingly interested in the ethics of food and eating and the entirely socially acceptable practices of animal cruelty in the name of food production.

It has taken me the best part of three decades to unlearn some of my distorted behaviour around food and eating and to notice how I used food in ways other than for nutrition. I picked up much more about body image, the ideal weight, and 'good' and 'bad' foods, rather than nutrition and how to eat: eat when you're hungry and stop when you're belly starts to tell you it's full. Eat what you're body wants to eat, rather than what your head is craving or what's on the adverts. Eat a balanced diet and don't snack between meals. Eat because you're hungry, rather than because you're sad and alone. Grow your own food so you really appreciate all the conditions it takes for a French bean to appear. The rules are quite simple in theory but so much harder in practice if you've grown up in an environment of charged confusion.

Understanding eating seems to be a lifelong voyage and interest. Last year, recovering from a debilitating virus, I completely lost my appetite. I didn't want to eat and felt sick. I listened to my body, and my body told me what to eat. Mouthful by mouthful, I started eating again - although, I found my taste for caffeine and sugar dropped away. In that phase I realised, perhaps for the first time, that I could eat exactly what I wanted to eat. How embarrassingly obvious, yet it hadn't been at all obvious to me until that moment, despite the work I've done. This powerful realisation was helped by the care of my partner who would nip to the shops to buy whatever my body wanted. I was spoilt and nurtured like never before.

These days I'm happy to inhabit a middle-aged body. I care more about what I put into my body and how much sleep I get rather than burning energy worrying endlessly about how I mightn't measure up to someone elses' image of female beauty. This middle-aged body has a few battle scars, but we're no longer at war. I love it more than I ever have before, and I love the fact that me and my body's storehouse of experiences are able to support others in getting into fuller relationship with their own embodied experience in healing wounds. And I'm on good terms with my Mum; she does her thing, and I do mine (and she's a great proof reader. Hi Mum!)

Where food comes from matters to me more than ever before. I don't want to eat food that costs the earth, even though I do, at times, indulge with the odd exotic fruit. I love growing our own vegetables and fruit, seeing directly the link between seed, plant, harvest, compost, and relishing the taste, texture, and nutritional value of something freshly picked or dug up, with earth still clinging to its roots. I am so appreciative that I have fresh food to eat and see more clearly the overused phrase that we are what we eat. I'm more aware of the 'hungry gap' during the productive year which once upon a time would have caused hunger and suffering to our ancestors and still causes suffering to fellow human beings living in poverty.

Learning how to eat and learning how to feel safe and nourished are vital for a healthy human life; yet, it feels like many of our societies are disordered in our individual and collective approach to food and nourishment. This reminds me of what's known as the 'hungry ghost' realm from the image of the Tibetan Wheel of Life. Hungry ghosts are creatures with huge, distended, empty bellies. They are said to be constantly hungry because their thin necks don't allow food to pass to their stomach. Food turns to fire and ash in their mouths. They keep seeking food and nourishment.

This desperate image reminds me of the current predicaments of Western societies. We are constantly craving and never seem happy or contented with our lot. Late stage capitalist habits of consumption compound this 'hungry ghost' pattern of addicted, compulsive behaviour. When the Buddha met a hungry ghost he is said to have offered it food and drink that was truly satisfying. This food and drink also symbolizes inner nourishment, taking the place of the inner emptiness of the 'hungry ghost'. But I am also aware of a growing body of people who want to live consciously, to live as simply, wisely, and as lovingly as they can in these uncertain times and not consuming the earth.

The Metta Sutta

If you know your own good
and know where peace dwells
then this is the task:

Lead a simple and a frugal life
uncorrupted, capable and just;
be mild, speak soft, eradicate conceit,
keep appetites and senses calm.

Be discreet and unassuming;
do not seek rewards.
Do not have to be ashamed
in the presence of the wise.

May everything that lives be well!
Weak or strong, large or small,
seen or unseen, here or elsewhere,
present or to come, in heights or depths,
may all be well.

Have that mind for all the world -
get rid of lies and pride -

a mother's mind for her baby,
her love, but now unbounded

Secure this mind of love,
no enemies, no obstructions
wherever or however you may be!It is sublime, this,

it escapes birth and death,
losing lust and delusion
and living in the truth!

References:
de Beauvoir, S. (2010) *The Second Sex*. Vintage.
Halse Anderson, L. (2014) *Winter Girls*. Marion Lloyd Books.
The Metta Sutta. The original 'Metta Sutta' can be found in the Suttanipāta (Sn 1.8) of the Pali Canon. This particular unpublished translation is by Dharmachari Vipassi.

9. Sheer Coincidences?

> Monks, suppose that this great earth were totally covered with water, and a man were to toss a yoke with a single hole there. A wind from the east would push it west, a wind from the west would push it east. A wind from the north would push it south, a wind from the south would push it north. And suppose a blind sea-turtle were there. It would come to the surface once every one hundred years. Now what do you think: would that blind sea-turtle, coming to the surface once every one hundred years, stick his neck into the yoke with a single hole?
>
> It would be a sheer coincidence, lord, that the blind sea-turtle, coming to the surface once every one hundred years, would stick his neck into the yoke with a single hole.
>
> It's likewise a sheer coincidence that one obtains the human state (Thanissaro Bhikkhu, 1998).

I am a sea turtle swimming in deep, azure-blue sea. I can see the ocean floor below, enveloped in fine white sand. I am paddling from side to side, rocking gently, enjoying the glints of watery light from the sun's overhead rays. I swim towards a gap in a wall of smooth, dark, horizontal rock and take a good look, but decide not to swim through. I circle around, relishing the motion and rhythm of being and moving. We reach the end of the Craniosacral session and I'm a human again. As I get down from the bench I can feel every vertebrae of my spine - my back is tingling with life.

"Do turtles have spines?" I ask the Craniosacral therapist. "Yes, I think so", she replies.

Why choose to be born? How to be born? How to be a body? These questions have emerged repeatedly for me through doing different forms of bodywork and psychotherapy over the years. I witness, too, those early-formed, deeply-felt existential questions in the grappling of my clients, re-visiting over and over the mystery of how to be incarnate in the moment: living, breathing, in relationship with self, other and world. How this mystery relates to the very first moment of incarnation, and before that, the detonation of conception. This morning, being the turtle and moving through that hole in the rock wall would have been venturing back into the watery, underworld soup of pre-conception. I stayed on this side of the wall, content enough to have been born, and happy enough, it seemed, to be a sea-turtle for a while, rather than a human, experimenting with paddling rather than walking, and enjoying the strength and protection of my strong, curved shell.

The opening excerpt about the sea-turtle is one of my favourite Buddhist texts, taken from the Chiggala Sutta (Thanissaro Bhikkhu, 1998). Not just because I am a great admirer of turtles, but because when I read it I never fail to appreciate having been born here and now, given the odds. At the moment I'm midway through an eighteen-month training in pre- and peri-natal psychology. I am trying to remember from our last residential the statistic we were given as to the odds of being born, alive and well. I can't remember it, but I know it was pretty startling, making the sea-turtle and yoke story sound not as fantastical as it might on first hearing.

I'm struck by memories from the work we have done on the residential workshops so far and how birth experiences vary enormously. Mine is a star-gazing birth. I'm absolutely determined to get out of a tight spot. I'm having to move very quickly, until I become stuck and breathless, struggling until my turtling head finds its way. Between times I gaze back up at the stars longingly, deciding whether to stay or go. It's incredibly painful and I'm largely alone, until the arrival of cold, clasping forceps yanking me out, creating a wave of startle through me and my mother's bodies. Other births are slow and sedate, with near divine connection between mum and child, others are drugged, some are stuck to the point of danger and are suddenly exited via a caesarean section.

The one thing all births have in common is that they mark the immense cusp between worlds: the enormity of a new life, the irrevocable changing of relationships between people and people - history in the making. It's painful, bloody, joyous, mysterious, welcomed, feared, celebrated, connecting and so common place. Yet in society so few of us pay attention to our arrival on earth, in particular, the experience of the baby. Imagine, we spend more time talking about the weather—especially those of us who are British!—than we do telling our birth stories or perhaps, even believing that we know, in our bodies, the story of our birth. What a strange thing indeed.

The same is true of death stories in our culture. I remember back to my father's sudden death and the importance of telling his death story and my part in it, as a way of grieving and giving shape to what had happened. I wrote it in minute detail, detective-like, and told it to the handful of friends who were up for listening, understanding the importance of the telling. Death, whether dying takes four years, four hours or four minutes, is the last part of someone's life, and is as valid and significant as any other part as they return to the life-death threshold.

So it is with birth. Our arrival is so significant in shaping who we become, and who we are right this moment becoming, yet aside from knowing where we were born, our weight, and perhaps how our name was chosen, we often know little else about our births. Perhaps this is a British thing, with bodily functions still being a bit taboo in polite conversation. Perhaps it's because of the increasing medicalization of birth which means it has largely been taken from the community into the often impersonal and transitory world of the hospital or medicalized setting. Perhaps it's because many of us no longer have lifestyles which permit the time and space to stop and breathe and be together around the time of a birth, or no longer have such close kinship ties. Whatever the causes, this phenomena surprises me. I have friends who don't even know in what phase of the day they were born.

It hasn't been like this for me - I've been curious about birth since I can remember, and perplexed that it isn't that way for others. Having said that, part of my fascination has been about making sense of my tricky arrival. I was born into shocking grief, so I've spent years untying knots: disentangling my mother's grief from my own grief, knowing the stories of my grandfather's sudden departure and my sudden arrival, and how they collided, and learning more latterly the story of my birth told to me in detail by my body rather than the family story of being a troublesome baby. And feeling the terrible loss of never having met either of my grandfathers.

It seems strange for me to be writing about birth psychology at this particular point in my life, given that I'm spending much of my time contemplating and writing about choosing *not* to have children. I'm completing my second book, *Other than Mother: Choosing Childlessness with Life in Mind*, exploring conscious decision-making in deciding to remain childfree and supporting others in their decision-making process (see Kamalamani, 2016). It's a hot topic and, in my mind, a really important and under-discussed one. What I most want to do is to create more dialogue in how we value life - in choosing whether to have children and in how we are more careful in how we live and work in the earth, our home. Of course, the common factor of both this piece about birth psychology and *Other than Mother* is the preciousness of life. It's no wonder that people want to keep having children - life is precious and new life is irresistible.

Birth psychology excites me, I realise, because it's never too late to re-pattern our relationship with our own birth story. Conception happens, our birth happened, we're here, and we never stop having opportunities to arrive more and more fully in our bodies and our experience through doing birth work, and in living the precious lives we've been given. The more in-depth I study my own birth and hold that work for fellow trainees, the more adept I am at recognising 'baby language' with clients and supervisees, noticing stuckness which echoes with birth experience, giving me clues as to how best to work. I can't help thinking that the more I know about my own birth story, the smoother will be my psychic passage out of this particular life. But who's to know?

> Death is not extinguishing the light; it is putting out the lamp because the dawn has come (Rabindranath Tagore, the Indian writer and philosopher, 1861-1941).

References:
Kamalamani. (2016) *Other than Mother: Choosing Childlessness with Life in Mind.* Earth Books, an imprint of John Hunt Publishing, Hampshire, UK.
Thanissaro Bhikkhu (1998) (translator) 'Chiggala Sutta: The Hole'. Translated from the Pali by Thanissaro Bhikku. SN 56.48 , PTS: S v 456, CDB ii 1872. Source:
http://www.accesstoinsight.org/tipitaka/sn/sn56/sn56.048.than.html Accessed 1/10/14

10. Meditating with Character

"It must be really anchoring to practise a faith"

"Oh you meditate, that's why you're so calm"

"Retreats must be so peaceful, I'd go - if only I had the time"

I chuckle to myself when I hear these well-meant comments from new friends when they discover that I practise Buddhism. In response: I find that anchoring comes and goes; I'm calm in the way that a swan looks calm, paddling like mad beneath the smooth, unruffled surface of the water. And, yes, I suggest we all make time to go on retreat, so long as we're prepared to cherish boredom and all the other experiences that will happen along. Rather than being anchoring, practising Buddhism and meditating have been more akin to having an invisible depth charge planted in the middle of me.

Right now, Buddhism and meditation are on trend, and it is likely that there are more folk meditating and practising - particularly mindfulness - in the 'western world' than ever before. Which, of course, is great news. Except that misconceptions abound about what meditation and practice are. The dangers of 'spiritual bypassing' (Welwood, 2000) are as present as ever, with spiritual practice having the potential to be yet another drug of choice; a realm in which we run the risk of seeking escapism and fantasy, near enemies indeed. Welwood coined the phrase 'spiritual bypassing' in noticing the tendency of western spiritual seekers to use spiritual ideas and practices to "avoid dealing with their emotional unfinished business" (Welwood, 2000, pp 5).

After 20 years of sitting on the cushion, or more honestly, struggling to get to the cushion (sitting's the easier part), I can still find myself magically on my feet with the kettle on in a split second. I am more appreciative of the messiness of meditation and the simple, beautiful, complexity of the Dharma—the teachings of the Buddha— than ever before. Being taught to meditate was the most valuable thing I've learnt, second only to watching myself try every tool in my extensive tool box in avoiding meditation and practice.

To draw upon the language of Wilhelm Reich (see Reich, 1990) we meditate and practice *in character*. That's likely to mean that part of us longs to meditate and practise, the other part's running in the opposite direction. Bringing together character structure and meditation practice is profound in understanding the messier and out-of-bounds bits of our experience and embodiment. This fascination with the interface between meditation, the Dharma, and neo-Reichian character structure was what lead me to write my first book *Meditating with Character* (Kamalamani, 2012). The grand irony was that I spent three years doing far more writing about meditation than actually meditating. There's always a catch . . .

My most familiar characterological strategies are to ping between my top and tail, head and pelvis: either distracting myself in the world of analytical thinking and existential questioning, or bouncing around, entertaining myself and the world, being endlessly and tirelessly fascinating. I distract myself with fantastically complex questions about the nature of existence - a Buddhist speciality, especially with all those lists of teachings. Or entertaining myself whilst bringing to mind the Buddha upon whom I meditate, running a full colour Blu Ray quality film rather than engaging with the koans of form and emptiness, self and other, and self and no self.

I've learned about the simple bliss of making contact with my experience through meditation and character structure. My 'heady' part can now more easily dissolve into the ease of just sensing the softening of the scalp. In fleeting flashes, there is no me or mine in the way I conceive of me or mine in my every day thinking. There's just this body, sitting and noticing sensations arise and fall, nothing to do, nowhere to go. A sigh on the out breath as my shoulders drop a few millimetres and I soften into the earth.

The facet of my character which longs to be entertaining inwardly cries out at the relief of being quiet; no audience, no performance, nor rush. The only job is to be enchanted by the ordinary awesomeness of the body and breath. I relish the texture of the breath, how its movement brushes my clothes against my body. It rolls on, no pushing or pulling, no beginning or end. Occupying this sense of being a body, even though there's nothing to occupy apart from sensations, feelings, thoughts, and even they keep changing. Fear arising as I have no one to entertain but myself, breathing into that fear, surrounding that fear with warmth if I can, I settle and feel an unclenching deep within myself.

In truth, after 20 years of meditation and practice, I often feel more anchored and calm, but those have arisen as much from the struggles and messiness of staying with my experience as the moments of bliss and inspiration. My experience of meditating with character has been that it's hard to spiritually by-pass anything, because you are more likely to witness what you're doing, as you do it, becoming more aware of your armouring, little by little. Not comfortable, maybe, but growthful. Spiritual practice – whatever that is - has to pay attention to embodiment, else it probably isn't spiritual practice. Meditation and embodied practice offer us an amazing doorway into the heart of the furnace of seeing how our characters were formed from pre-conception to the present day - and how character can change in the furnace's heat. To enter so deeply into our habits and strategies, our views and beliefs, that we come out the other side and wonder what the fuss was all about. Until, of course, we encounter the next layer of habits and strategies, views and beliefs . . . (and holding lightly to it all).

Being a Dharma practitioner feels like being an archaeologist, as does practising body psychotherapy. In my practice of embodied spirituality, the theme of this edition of *Somatic Psychotherapy Today*, I sift layer upon layer of interesting sediment and different rock strata, each with their historical era and particular properties.

We can easily think that the strata are fossilised - character armouring can feel so solid and immoveable - but so often that's the story of the clutter of the mind and not the story of the integrating body-mind and the story it has to tell when we listen-in with care, patience, and a growing capacity to dialogue with the multitudes of parts of ourselves, and hopefully, interested others.

The spiritual life is a warrior's path, so they say. Not necessarily because it has to involve noble quests, sword fights, or long nights of the soul - although those seem to happen at various stages - but because it takes training, discipline, persistence, tenacity, a sense of humour, a leap of faith, and an appreciation of the absurd to keep on going. Of course, it's also an ordinary path. More than anything these days my practice also relies upon leaving from time to time the built, grey world of surfaces and straight lines to encounter greener pathways and hedges; where bird song is louder than human chatter. Where I'm more likely to hear the meow of the cat stalking me, and the rippit of a frog looking for a twilight mate rather than the shrieks of the police sirens. Where I touch soil and weeds rather than keyboard and phone. It's a relief to remember, in these precious moments, that humanity is but one species of life on earth.

I move through the landscape and the landscape moves me. I strike the balance between moving and sitting; not moving enough leads to tightness, constriction, and rusty joints, whilst meditation calls for looseness, expansion, and fluidity. Embodied spirituality doesn't makes sense to me unless I remember my place in the other-than-human world. I can't explain that in words, but luckily Carl Jung can, and did, way before me:

> For it is the body, the feeling, the instincts, which connect us with the soil. If you give up the past you naturally detach from the past; you lose your roots in the soil, your connection with the totem ancestors that dwell in the soil. You turn outward and drift away, and try to conquer other lands because you are exiled from your own soil (Jung in Sabini, 2002: 73).

So, as we practise, may we love the mess as much as we love the inspiration, remember our uniqueness as well as our similarity with all our living beings, and practise hard whilst we simultaneously lighten up and cackle at the absurdity of it all. In the first decade of practice I was seeking meaning in things. In the second decade I was practising so as to meet fully the world as I find it. Let's see what the third decade brings. In the words of a respected friend and colleague, Jungian Analyst, professor, and public intellectual, Andrew Samuels:

> I seek to advance a vision of spirituality that is regular, ubiquitous and permeates every aspect of existence. It is not intended to be a lofty, exhortative, sermonising approach. Quite the opposite. My take on spirituality discerns its worm-like nature, not its eagle-like nature. Spirituality as an underneath as well as an over the top thing. And because approaches to spirituality so easily go over the top, it is often better to stay underneath (Samuels, 2002).

References:
Jung, C. (1988). *Zarathustra Seminar*. Edited by James Jarrett. Princeton, NJ: Princeton University Press. Page 1541. Quoted in Sabini, M. (2002) (ed.) *C.G. Jung on Nature, Technology & Modern Life*. North Atlantic Books. Page 73.
Kamalamani. (2012). *Meditating with Character*. Mantra Books, an imprint of John Hunt Publishing, Hampshire, England. See chapter 6 for an introduction to post-Reichian character positions.
Reich, W. (1990) *Character Analysis*. Third edition. Farrar, Straus and Giroux (FSG), New York, USA.
Samuels, A. (2002). 'A New Anatomy of Spirituality: Clinical and Political Demands the Psychotherapist Cannot Ignore'. 'A lightly edited version of a lecture given in the series 'Psychotherapy and Spirituality' at the London Centre for Psychotherapy on 26

October 2002'. Accessed from http://www.andrewsamuels.com accessed 5/6/13.

Welwood, J. (2000). *Towards a Psychology of Awakening: Buddhism, Psychotherapy and the Path of Personal and Spiritual Transformation*. Shambhala Publications Inc. USA.

11. The Burning House

Once upon a time, many years ago, there was a wealthy man living in a huge old house. He lived in this house with hundreds of his children, and many other beings of all shapes and sizes. The house was vast, but it only had one front door. And although he was a wealthy man, this huge house was rather tumble down; decaying in parts. Now one day the man was sitting in the garden when he noticed that a fire had broken out in the house. The man was, understandably, very concerned for his children playing inside. "Flee, flee!" he yelled. But, of course, being young, they were completely absorbed in their games and toys and they ignored him – I'm sure that's a very familiar feeling for many of you parents. All the while, the house was being consumed by dancing flames and the crackling and falling of beams and wreckage.

The wealthy man thought on his feet, coming up with the perfect way of luring the children from the burning house so that they would come to no harm. Knowing that they were fond of interesting playthings, he called out to them, "Listen! Outside the gate are the carts that you have always wanted: carts pulled by goats, carts pulled by deer, and carts pulled by oxen. Come out and play with them!" The wealthy man knew that these things would be irresistible to his children.

The children, eager to play with these new toys, rushed out of the house excitedly. Instead of the carts that he had promised, the father gave them a cart much better than anything he had described - a cart draped with precious stones and pulled by white bullocks. The children were so happy, and the man was so glad the children were safe, as the house burned to the ground.

This parable of the burning house is adapted from a traditional Buddhist text called the 'White Lotus Sutra' (see Soothill, 1987). It is all about the human predicament, and may well be familiar to some of you. The burning house represents the burning of the 'fires' of old age, sickness and death, traditionally known as the first three of the 'four sights' in Buddhism. The kindly father represents the teachings of the Buddha; encouraging the children to leave the pleasures of playing with their toys for the greater pleasure of enlightenment; being fully awake, being the complete embodiment and quintessence of wisdom and kindness. (These days, of course, the tempting toys might have to be iPads, Barbie dolls, PlayStation and the like, but hopefully you get my drift!)

The father is very skilful in how he lures the children from the house. He doesn't nag them, or shout at them, or get in a complete flap so he's unable to take care of them. He stays calm and realises what will attract and fascinate the children based on what they love. In Buddhist jargon, he uses 'skilful means' in helping his children leave the house safely and without panic.

This parable leapt out at me when I realised I wanted to write about the trauma of everyday life in 2015, in response to this edition's theme of trauma. Not only is it one of my favourite parables, but it seems particularly fitting in the challenges we face in the world at present. From a Buddhist point of view, the world is always 'on fire', as it were. Those of us who are the metaphorical children—in that we are not enlightened every moment—are habitually caught up in the 'games' of everyday life, tending to act more readily from greed, hatred and delusion, than contentment, loving kindness (traditionally known in Buddhism as 'metta'), and wisdom. We tend to live as if things are permanent, substantial and satisfactory. We are surprised when things end, when we become ill, when friends or family members die, despite being in a constant cycle of life and death in our own lives and in the changing seasons around us.

This parable is clever in using the image of a house as its main image. Our houses, our homes, are, quite understandably, sought after places of peace and security. In fact, our homes, too, are on fire! Hopefully they are places of sanctuary and rest. They also decay, need work and aren't immune from tornadoes, subsidence, burglars, and, in some places, bombings. These things which we imagine will offer us security in some fixed, unchanging sense, can, in fact, be a source of great suffering, exacerbated by our delusional views about what makes us happy and a notion of lasting security in life.

There is a huge amount we could talk about around this parable and its different meanings. I would like to draw out the metaphor of the house as the interrelated world crises at present; a world in which global temperatures are rising, climate chaos is upon us, sea ice is melting, and environmental degradation is a sad fact of life. We are inflicting an unprecedented degree of harm upon other-than-human life, with us being in what is known as the sixth extinction crisis, with the United Nations Environment Programme estimating that between 150 and 200 species of plant, insect, bird and mammal become extinct every hour (Vidal, 2010).

So the human predicament causes great harm, not only to our personal well-being, but in terms of causing harm to the planet, our home, which ultimately causes harm to us, given the interrelationship of the ecosystem. And, all the while, the majority of the world's population are carrying on as if nothing's happening, as if it's business as normal. It is fairly common place for us to live our lives as if there were two, three, four, or five planets, rather than the one of which we are a part. In fact, it's a challenge to live a life as if there's only one planet, even if you give up flying, go vegetarian or vegan, have one or no children, and recycle, given the carbon footprint assigned to each of us on behalf of the carbon footprint of governments on our behalf (the military, health, infrastructure etc.)

Still, it's worth trying to clean up our individual acts. I've had the recent good fortune to train as a 'carbon conversations' (1) facilitator, holding a space for anyone concerned about climate change and carbon reduction to come along and understand their own powerful and ambivalent responses to the subject, supporting them to make practical changes, and understand the need for political and social change (Randall & Brown, 2015, iv). It was great, supportive, inspiring, and sobering. Great to take action in the face of themes that can be over-whelming and provoke horrified anxiety. Supportive to work with such an interesting and engaged group of people with similar interests in common. Inspiring to see that others care about the world and you're not the only one holding this seemingly dirty secret that the world's on fire and yet the majority of folk are carrying on as normal (the famous 'keep calm and carry on' motivational poster comes to mind, from World War Two). And sobering to see the size of the task in hand for all of us.

When I heard that this fall edition was to be about trauma approaches what was uppermost in my mind - a recurring theme for me - was how can we, as body psychotherapists, make our mark here? I know I'm not alone in having clients who are becoming more and more affected by the reality of, and denial, of climate change. These clients aren't necessarily all that environmentally aware - some are and some aren't. But they're affected anyway. How can we not be affected by what's going on, when we are part of a system which is condoning loss and destruction? Where can we voice our fear, pessimism, as well as kindle and re-kindle our 'active hope' (Macy & Johnstone, 2012)? I am reminded of the words of Stephanie Mills:

> Among do-gooders, it is bad form to be a pessimist, but I cannot seem to get that extinction crisis out of my mind. Or that population explosion. Or global climate change. Or the consequences of an era of trade agreements. Can't get those billionaires; those landless, homeless, jobless billions; those new diseases; that

global casino of finance capitalism; the corporate capture of the media; those aging nuclear reactors; those surveillance satellites; those crowded prisons out of my mind (Mills, 2002: 28).

Personally I long to be part of a body of therapists who do their bit in embodying the father in the 'burning house' parable. We can recognise that the house is on fire (rather than stay in the house, playing, tempting though that is, with all the play things on offer in our lifestyles...) and we can offer the support, awareness and challenge to others to leave the burning house. As body psychotherapists we are well placed to do this, aren't we? So many of us understand intimately the nature of trauma. Intimately in terms of many of our personal experiences, and in the hundreds and thousands of hours we have spent with clients and supervisees in working with, talking about, and reflecting on trauma. Working ourselves in therapy and offering that holding to our clients in visiting those out-of-reach places of terror in facing the unfaceable, feeling what's been frozen, speaking the forbidden, so we can live now in a body which is more alive and more present. We are well versed in holding transformative spaces, in being with the unthinkable and unfeelable.

Perhaps one reason why more of us aren't more vocal in sharing what we know and making our mark far beyond the therapy room is because we are, in the words of Jungian Analyst Jerome Bernstein: 'borderlander personalities'. We are in touch with what he calls 'transrational reality'. He defines that as:

> objective nonpersonal, nonrational phenomena
> occurring in the natural universe, information and
> experience that does not readily fit into standard cause
> and effect logical structure (Bernstein, 2005: xv).

Bernstein points out how many of us wouldn't be able to function without this connection, and yet, in parallel, feel forced to conceal that dimension of our experience, even from our closest people, through fear of being ostracized and seeming odd. Add to that the size of the grief in many of our hearts, as we begin the process of acknowledging the harm we're causing as a species, and it's understandable that's it very challenging to contemplate 'making our mark' given that it means dwelling in and being with the most difficult of emotions.

If we are able to adopt the skilful means represented by the father in the burning house, not only do we ourselves stop sleep-walking towards catastrophe, but also carefully encourage others to look at their strategies of choice in the face of climate change, which may include hedonism, immense terror, overwhelm, freeze, disavowal, and, of course, denial. It's far from easy work, in fact, right now, it is sadly still counter-cultural. But then, practising as a body psychotherapist isn't easy work, so at least we are used to a challenge. Added to that, our brains are hardwired to ignore climate change - see Marshall's excellent book on this theme 'Don't even think about it: Why our brains are wired to ignore climate change', Marshall, 2014.

I guess we can 'keep calm and carry on' in the burning house, playing the game of business as normal. Or we can 'keep calm and carry on' knowing that whether or not climate change is reversible, whether or not the destructive ways of our species has already gone too far, we are living a simple life as fully as possible - for life is surely what this is all about! - and doing what we can in raising awareness, taking action, making changes and remembering that humans are but one life form on planet earth. In our therapy work, I wonder what would happen if we all held in mind the earth and other-than-human and more-than-human life, whether we work in a high rise block or in a converted shed in the wilds? Can we dare to make our mark, having the difficult conversations with family and friends about our own decisions to curb our carbon footprint? Can we bear to check out how the anthropocentricism of our world seeps into our therapy work and to bring more of a whole earth, ecological perspective?

Note:
(1) 'Carbon Conversations' originated in work pioneered by Rosemary Randall, Andy Brown and Shilpa Shah during 2005-7 for the Akashi project and for the charity Cambridge Carbon Footprint. The project arose from the conjunction of Rosemary's work as a psychotherapist and her prior background in creating distance learning materials for the Open University in the UK. Carbon Conversations developed into a programme of six, fortnightly, friendly, practical groups that help participants to face climate change. See: http://www.carbonconversations.org/home

References:
Bernstein, J.S. (2005). *Living in the Borderland: The Evolution of Consciousness and the Challenge of Healing Trauma*. New York: Routledge.
Macy, J., & Johnstone, C. (2012). *Active Hope: How to Face the Mess We're In Without Going Crazy*. Novato, California: New World Library.
Marshall, G. (2014). *Don't Even Think About It: Why Our Brains Are Wired To Ignore Climate Change*. New York: Bloomsbury.
Mills, S. (2002). *Epicurean Simplicity*. CA: A Shearwater Book, Island Press.
Randall, R., & Brown, A. (2015). *In Time For Tomorrow? The Carbon Conversations Handbook*. Stirling, Scotland: The Surefoot Effect.
Soothill, W. E. (1987). *The Lotus of the Wonderful Law or the Lotus Gospel*. Richmond, Surrey:
Curzon Press Ltd.
Vidal, J. (2010). 'UN Environment Programme: 200 Species Extinct Every Day, Unlike Anything Since Dinosaurs Disappeared 65 Million Years Ago', Huffington Post, 17/8/2010.

12. Terrorized Bodies

I was in Paris on November 13th 2015—the evening when ISIL's bombs and shootings terrorized the city and its northern suburb of Saint-Denis. My partner and I had spent the day wandering; one of those rare, precious days when you're lucky enough to be with the one you love and haven't seen for a few weeks, in a favorite city abounding with memories. We were in no rush—meandering and seeing where our feet took us, enjoying the mild, autumnal weather, mingling with other tourists and locals. By evening we decided to have an early dinner and head home. Thank goodness for the disappointing meal we had. Thank goodness for our tired feet that took us home early. Thank goodness that we didn't carry on walking—we were only a few blocks from where the shootings and bombings occurred a little later.

The following morning as we read on the internet the official advice to stay indoors, I was struck by my fury and bloody-minded defiance, quickly replacing the agony I initially felt. I determinedly wanted to get out and about on the streets of Paris as soon as possible. No one would keep me indoors in some strange curfew! I'm so used to, and privileged by, feeling free. The look of shock on the faces of passers-by brought me back to earth, as did my deep fear and the fear in the air. Later we admitted we were both scared getting on the tube, not least when two guys leapt over the barrier to avoid buying a ticket. They laughed and shouted "allahu akbar". Not terrorists. Two local lads messing about on a tense day. Maybe messing about, maybe having a dig in response to the racism they most likely routinely experience.

It was a solemn Saturday, as you might imagine. I would rather have been home, truth be told, under a blanket on the sofa with tea. But we weren't going to leave Paris, because it wouldn't have felt right (and look - we're still alive). The joy of the previous day was a million miles away. There were moments of feeling, what is it? Survivor guilt? We could so easily have been killed. Why not me, as much as why me? Acts of 'terror' put me in touch with that yawning sense of powerlessness. None of us are safe in the face of people prepared to blow themselves up for their cause. And, of course, it's so easy to over-amplify the danger we're in. But people die and will die. They/we aren't just statistics; we're real beings with blood in our veins. It could be any of us: black, white, Muslim, Buddhist.

My partner and I found ourselves wandering past the cordoned-off Bataclan theatre at dusk to lay flowers. We had visited the Pere-Lachaise cemetery, a trip planned before the bombings and shootings, and our feet took us toward central Paris, wanting to gather together. I felt none of the rage of the morning, but baffled and moved. Baffled by the scene ahead of us: on one side of the road a media circus of broadcasting TV crews, vans, satellite dishes and blinding spot lights. On the other, a solemn shrine of flowers, candles, hand-written messages and people paying respectful homage. A young man, no older than 25, in his hoodie and jeans walked towards the bank of flowers, stopped, and knelt on his right knee with his face bowed to the bustling pavement for minutes on end. His small dog to his right stood stock still. I wept.

Reading Facebook the next day I felt my crushing limitations. Some friends were questioning why other friends were changing their profile picture to the French flag. How come, they asked, they didn't change their Facebook picture when other countries were bombed, like Lebanon or Kenya? They had a good point. I'd already decided to change my Facebook photo to the symbol of the CND peace symbol in the shape of the Eiffel tour, which I saw, Sunday morning, chalked on the pavement near the metro in Montmartre. Peace is the only answer - if only we had an inkling of a collective notion of how to achieve it, let alone really realising that it starts with us. I felt the limitations of my own empathy. I'm more moved by the aftermath of violence in Paris than in Lebanon.

I'm not proud of it all, but it's better to admit it and work with my preference and prejudice then pretend otherwise.

I love Paris; I have friends and memories here. I speak more French than any language other than English. Hell, I even dreamt in French once, a moment I cling to when I'm questioning my linguistic abilities. Feeling my limitations and lack of imagination and universal empathy has been humbling after 21 years of practising loving-kindness meditation. It also feels vitally important, in the spirit of emotional honesty, to know where I am, to face myself as I look in the post-Paris mirror. It reminds me of the last time I felt most personally effected by a terrorist attack, flying to Kenya on September 12th 2001, where I then worked as an aid worker. It was bizarre walking through an abandoned, Marie-Celeste (1) like Schipol Airport in Amsterdam, all the TV screens turned off lest we lose our appetite for boarding an airplane that day.

It was horrific getting on a virtually empty plane, remembering all those people turned to human bombs 24 hours earlier. It was sobering turning up in an edgy Kenya, its capital Nairobi having been shaken by bombing only a few years earlier, with hundreds killed and thousands injured. It was a useful reminder to hear the voice of the Somalia cab driver: "Eh, the deaths are terrible, and the American government have had it coming". Our/my western freedoms have come at quite a cost.

Mulling over the theme of this edition of *Somatic Psychotherapy Today*: 'the Embodied Self in a Dis-Embodied Society', I initially felt it was a gift in terms of having a mirror held up to my experience as I felt in turn: horror, rage, revenge, terror, compassion, sorrow, and a new stillness of not knowing (I even felt joy, particularly arriving home at St Pancras station in London, but it feels a bit crass mentioning that which I know, too, is a wrong view).

The weeks that followed the Paris attacks I felt incredibly embodied and disembodied. Feeling the sorrow of the heart and the size of the suffering in the world, I fully occupy this thing I call 'my' body. Imagining what I would like to do to the guys with the guns shooting at the audience in the Bataclan theatre I felt myself tighten, changing to icy steel, dissociating from my heart or, in fact, any shred of warmth. A moment later I felt ashamed and a flooding of too many feelings to bear: shame, guilt, am I a terrorist too, then? My nephew, lead singer in a rock band, and his mates, frequent places like the Bataclan. I do, too, as it happens, supporting them, but that Saturday, it was them and the younger generation most on my mind. Thinking of their lives being taken is far worse than imagining the taking of my own.

At this point, however, I can't make sense of a distinction between an embodying or disembodying self and an embodying or disembodying world. We are all the world, we are all a curious mix of embodied and disembodied.

I arrived in Paris having travelled from Ecodharma, a fabulous teaching centre and community in Catalunya, in the region of Lleida in the Pyrenees, where I had been part of a facilitation team fortunate enough to be working with activists and change-makers. Ecodharma is located in a beautiful, wild horse-shoe shaped valley of limestone ridges, pine forests, huge rocks presiding over the vista and pillows of shale in the valley floor. It is a place where my body stops and rests, as I find myself gazing in awe at the vultures above, the sky, and the changing light reflecting on the rock's craggy, vertical, surfaces. It was hard leaving that valley and community, my heart open and full and sad until the next time. I had a fabulous fortnight in that place, working with like-minded people wanting to create a better world, a more embodied, related world.

Thus, my decision in the aftermath of mountain-living and a weekend in Paris is to stay engaged, continue to work at fabulous, world-changing places like Ecodharma, support my clients in finding their feet and the rest of their agency. I also want to stop and relish life, doing the stuff that matters which isn't work-related.

May terror never fossilize in our hearts and stop us loving and acting with and for the world. And may our resistance be the resistance of a soft, open heart.

Note:
(1) The Marie Celeste was a ship that was found years after a trip was abandoned. It was afloat and found just as it had been left.

13. Diversity

Not long after I qualified as a therapist, I had a dream. I wanted to create a shop-fronted organisation on my local high Street (1) to offer drop-in counseling and psychotherapy services. It was easy to imagine given that Gloucester Road, my local high Street in North Bristol, is well-known in the UK for being a high Street boasting a high percentage of independently owned and run shops - sadly now relatively unusual in the UK. It wouldn't be a bad location either; not the poorest nor the poshest area of town, with a strong community focus. Accessible, popular, not as intimidating as some Bristol suburbs can be with their visible wealth.

To tell you the truth, the dream extended beyond my local high Street. I envisioned drop-in centres in all towns and cities in the UK - maybe even beyond! A place for people to seek support in a 'normalised' setting. Now this wasn't simply a therapy centre for private practitioners to hire rooms. No, I imagined a beautiful space, a welcoming place for people of all backgrounds. A gathering and meeting place for anyone and everyone to network and gather information.

> Psychotherapy is rooted in an ethos and devotion to the common good. It asks us to examine the processes of self-deception that perpetuate individual unhappiness and social structures that are inequitable and oppressive. Yet psychotherapy has for the most part been a white, privileged profession, hence training and treatment has focused on this population (Ellis, 2016: 11).

I envisioned a building located in the heart of the community. The centre's staff and occupants could maintain contact with city-wide specialised local counselling services, training institutions, and with local doctor's surgeries and hospitals. Group meeting rooms, individual therapy rooms, and a comprehensive library and resource centre were designed with people in mind. Spaces would be created where people might make themselves a drink whilst browsing and meeting others.

In this centre, diversity was reflected in the type of counseling and psychotherapy offered from different modalities and traditions, including body psychotherapy being made more visible. Folks could finally stop asking "what's that?" as the power of somatic work became more widely understood and accepted. Short-term work was to exist alongside long term work, rather than the current preoccupation and prioritizing of cognitive behavioural therapy and short-termism in the UK government's preferred approaches. Seeking therapy had the potential to become commonplace, as acceptable and as affordable as going to the post office or buying bread or carrots.

Of course, a significant shift needs to occur for this dream to manifest. Therapy still isn't, in the UK at least, as ordinary, as acceptable and as affordable as buying bread or carrots. In its public provision, it's caught up with economics and the prevailing agendas of the medical profession and the increasingly market-driven professionalization of the mainstream therapy membership bodies.

There are still taboos around seeking therapy in the UK; maybe the taboos are less of an issue in the USA? Many people can't afford therapy nor even know where to begin in finding a therapist. Many don't realise that therapy might be useful and relevant to them. Therapy often isn't included in medical insurance cover. There are, thank goodness, many therapy services in Bristol offering low-cost and subsidised therapy, although these services tend to have increasingly long waiting lists and, by necessity, have tended to move to a model of short-term, solution-focused methods. Nothing wrong with those necessarily, except for when a client wants longer term therapy and given the limitations that exist when this sort of long term therapy is under increasing threat.

Those most at need at the edges of society tend to suffer most, as services are cut and services are run by often over-worked, dedicated staff trying to make ends meet and be present for their clients.

I dreamt that our care for one another's psychological and spiritual wellbeing was such a priority there was a solid presence in every town and city. If we can have bookmakers, coffee shops and insurance brokers, surely we can have therapy on the high street? This care and the existence of these centres would mean true 'care in the community' in the words of the system implemented during Margaret Thatcher's term as the UK's prime minister in 1983, treating and caring for differently abled people in their homes rather than in an institution (what actually happened in many cases is that the care simply failed to happen.)

In my dream therapists not only had the chance to practice in the city centre, but also to meet, join together and advocate for change. After all: 'Therapists are always expressing a political position - because their work always and inevitably flows from a view on how humans should be, and therefore carries a vision of how we could become and how we should be. However, these visions and positions are often implicit rather than explicit or even held out of consciousness' (Totton, 2012: 92).

So what happened to my dream? I got busy. My private practice slowly and surely filled up. And, I forgot it. Granted, I still do useful things, I hope. Apart from my paid work, I was a steering group member of Psychotherapists and Counsellors for Social Responsibility for many years and edited their journal. I continue to write, campaign, and teach, my attempts to raise awareness of things that matter. I also continue to do some pro-bono work and offer concessionary places, but this isn't the same as that dream.

Before I trained as a therapist, I was pretty sceptical about the therapy trade. I did the training determined to qualify; and yet, I knew that I might not end up practising as a therapist. I worried that it was something primarily catering to the anxious middle classes, even though I saw its very real potential for anyone and everyone. It's just that that potential seemed a bit hidden, certainly not accessible, and almost a bit 'hush, hush'. It also had a mystifying language of its own. I'm weary of mystifying languages when it means that it can limit access; although I am sure I'm guilty myself of falling into using jargon at times, it's hard not to. I sometimes witnessed others becoming a bit 'psycho-babbly' once they learned the new, sometimes rarefied language of therapy. It was a bit of a turn off.

I did become a therapist, and I love the work. But I'm not sure I lost all my scepticism. Not scepticism about much of the practice I see, or the dedication of the therapists around me, or the very real changes clients make in therapy. No, scepticism about how we collectively organise and provide facilities to support thriving mental and somatic health. In the 14 years I've been practising, the public provision of counseling and therapy has been in turmoil. I'm not employed by the National Health Service, and reports from friends and colleagues aren't heartening. And before long we mightn't even have a National Health Service anymore, following the American model.

Maybe therapy in private practice is even more inaccessible, not simply because of the investments in terms of costs and time involved, but because many folks don't necessarily know that counseling and therapy happen in private practice. Again, this might be different in the USA, maybe not. But for many, their local GP surgery (MD) is their first point of call.

I return to my dream. How can we re-imagine and bring places to life in our community where therapy is seen as a useful service that many of us might seek at one time or another? How can we help to re-locate so-called mental health and somatic health in our communities, networked both with the more conventional medical model service providers, as well as secular approaches to mindfulness, for example, and other faith or spiritual groups offering different approaches and methods that clients may find beneficial for their healing?

Community-located services are dying in the UK high street in all sorts of ways. Just the other day my partner and I stole away for a quick lunch in one of our favourite local cafés in a nearby suburb. We asked the lovely café owner how business was going. "Slow", he replied, shaking his head, "this is a dead street". My heart sank. It's true; it is a bit of a dead street. Most high streets are no longer frequented by grocers, butchers, greengrocers, hardware shops. These are now located out-of-town and are part of mega-stores. Libraries and post offices are even harder to come by.

So my dream of the high street drop-in centre may not be a reality in the times we are in. Or will it all go full circle? The trend of buying local, of farmers' markets filled with local produce and restaurants proud of their sourcing within a 50-mile radius are gaining popularity at the same time as the centralisation and digitalisation of so many services. Where does this leave us as practitioners? And as humans? And what does this mean for the future of therapy? Thankfully there are many organisations world-wide providing counseling and psychotherapy to those who mightn't otherwise access support. I know tens of such organisations in Bristol, and many more nation-wide. It's jaw-dropping what they manage to do on a shoe-string and under the pressure of constant worries about funding, spending a lot of time completing funding proposals for scarce charitable money and grants.

How can we sing out more the need for counseling and psychotherapy provision which is open to all?

How do we make our own private practice work more accessible?

What can we do to attract clients who might never have considered coming to therapy, for all sorts of reasons?

How can we keep the initiative in noticing our own blind spots and shortcomings, which might mean the work we do isn't as accessible as we'd hope, perhaps due to our own un-acknowledged class or colour or financial privilege, to name but a few privileges?

I love raising and mulling and acting on these questions. I love them because they were only minimally addressed in my initial qualifying training. Don't get me wrong, all the training I've been fortunate to have done has been sound, solid, careful, and rightfully challenging in terms of getting me to understand therapy and the role of a therapist and the therapeutic relationship and different models of therapy. Where my initial therapy education fell short was in exploring in more detail the contexts, the systems within which we operate—social, political, ecological, and economic considerations that have a direct impact not only on clients' day to day existence, but also on their likelihood of affording or knowing how to access therapy.

I long for the day when therapy is open to all, where support is not only accessed via the medical model. I also long for the day when somatic work is seen and respected on equal footing with other therapeutic approaches, knowing as we do its potential for deep and lasting transformation.

Note:
(1) High Street or the High Street is a metonym for the concept and frequently the street name of the primary business street of towns or cities in the UK. In the USA and Canada, the term used is Main Street. In a town, it implies the focal point for businesses, especially shops.

References:
Ellis, E. (2015). 'Updating psychotherapy training: Equality and diversity issues in psychotherapy training'. *The Psychotherapist.* Journal of the UKCP (UK Council for Psychotherapy).
Totton, N. (2012). *Not a Tame Lion: Writing on Therapy in its Social and Political Context.* PCCS Books, Ross-on-Wye, UK.

14. All at Sea

He allowed himself to be swayed by his conviction that human beings are not born once and for all on the day their mothers give birth to them, but that life obliges them over and over again to give birth to themselves (Márquez, 2007).

It is late afternoon and my friends and I are making our way along the beach connecting Polzeath and New Polzeath in North Cornwall. We have been wandering for hours. We check our watches—we're late—and start to run, joking, giddy with sugar highs from eating candy canes. We're suddenly in the midst of swirling tides, waves from all directions—not knowing whether they are coming or going—the strength of the undercurrent tugging at our ankles, the unforgiving rock face ahead of us too steep to scramble to safety. My senses are scrambled as I remember. Jokes are replaced with concerned yelps as we hop about trying to find shallow water and to avoid rocks. We piggy back the youngest of the party who starts to cry. It is unknown and suddenly dangerous; all the giddiness is gone. If we had been any later, we wouldn't have got through.

I am reminded of another watery memory I found myself recounting at a conference workshop I facilitated last weekend, also in Cornwall, this time at the world-renowned Eden project. I invited participants to tell their 'earth stories' through sharing glimpses of my own. I included images of particular landscapes and seascapes, animals and flora and fauna, which have been significant in my earth story, one of them being Trebarwith Strand, a shallow shelving beach barely 10 miles up the coast from Polzeath. I recounted body boarding here when I was 13 years old—one of my favourite things at the time—and being dragged off of my board, thrown head over heels and dragged along the sharp rocks of the sea bed. I emerged shocked and sobered, gladder than ever to catch my breath and to turn to see people on the shore's edge. I have always felt awe for the sea, and that day it was amplified, with the sore bruises across my hips and thighs cautioning me of the sea's strength.

> Birth memories, deeply hidden in the unconscious mind, usually announce themselves indirectly. They appear in association with some triggering event, such as watching people fall through space in a movie, seeing someone pinned down in a fight, or perhaps just watching a fish wriggling and struggling on a fishing line. The extreme feeling of anxiety stirred up by these events calls attention to the significance of the memory hiding at deeper levels of consciousness (Chamberlain, 1998: 92).

Birth memories often emerge in relationship to the sea for me, with its undercurrents, turning tides, rocks, and possible danger. Apparently, I have a very 'Neptunian' influence in my birth chart; I'm no astrologer, so I'm not sure what that means. Once I had recovered from my early terror of water and fear of disappearing down the plug hole when I was bathed—yes, really, much to the sadistic delight of my older brother, making sure I would be seated at the plug hole end whilst he sat back and enjoyed the drama...! I loved being in water and spent literally hours swimming, messing about, floating, body boarding. I think, for me, a triggering event, in Chamberlain's words, was recalling the body boarding memory at Trebarwith Strand.

Changing tides are the themes that emerge as I turn my attention towards engaging with this final print version of *Somatic Psychotherapy Today* about pre and peri-natal psychology. It is a timely theme, given that life has been punctuated by endings and beginnings of late. Four friends have died—three pretty suddenly—and I'm in the process of amicably leaving the

Buddhist movement and order of which I have been a part for the past 21 years. In June I finally started being treated for two long-standing chronic health issues, and I am feeling better and have much gratitude to the medical world, after, I confess, much ambivalence (we didn't get off to a good start—when I was on the final module of my pre and peri natal training I had one of my most profound and mightily unexpected spiritual experiences holding some high forceps in the palms of my hands as I might an objective of infinite value or beauty). It has been a phase of thresholds; the unknown and unknowable. I suppose that as things draw to a close, as people die, or even as we move between things, our earliest echoes—our experiences in the womb and birth canal—are evoked on a visceral, if subconscious level. No wonder I feel a bit stuck for words and all at sea as I attempt to string something together, which has a faint hope of making sense.

> "Let nothing disturb you
> Let nothing frighten you..."
> (St Teresa, see SPCK)

St Teresa of Avila counsels, wisely and helpfully, her words leaping off the page of the order of service at my friend's funeral last Friday week. Roy was my first spiritual teacher, the second vicar I met at my local parish church as a girl. It's uncanny to be reflecting on my early connections with spiritual practice and the stage I find myself in right now, leaving my spiritual home of more than two decades; a spiritual death of sorts. I hope that there will be some sort of spiritual rebirth after this in-between crepuscular space, but I can't know for sure.

What I do know is the beauty of the farewells I have been blessed to be part of this year. Two contrasting memories: Pete's funeral in a green Staffordshire valley on one of those days when summer makes an unexpected curtain call. An afternoon of Polish song, coming of age tales, belly laughs and copious tears. Roy's simple, quiet, touching funeral on a still, beautifully blue, cold, crisp, clear winter's day on a pretty Somerset hillside, still speckled with the last few red and golden autumn leaves clinging to their branches.

I've found myself much comforted by St Teresa's words. I realise I'm much comforted by them because they put me in mind of Roy. Years ago I visited Roy and his lovely wife, Winifred, herself an exemplar of deep faith, when Roy was vicar to British expatriates living on the Costa Blanca in Spain. We had been to the beach—sea and sand again—and I was fussing about the sand on my legs and feet; I'm not a big fan of sand between my toes. Roy looked at me, smiled, and said in his gently lilting Yorkshire, "oh don't worry love, your legs will soon dry and the sand will brush off, don't notice it for now". I have often remembered this incident when I've been stressed, and I've remembered it many times since Roy's passing. To him it was probably just a passing comment; to me it was kind, soothing words at just the right moment.

In the past few weeks most things have frightened me, although thankfully this phase is easing. In remembering and writing about Roy I feel like I have been reminded of my church-going roots and remembering what I left behind in my early teens. I am gladdened that there is a chapter on the 'Theological Paradigm' in Maret's 'The Prenatal Person' (1997), which I plan to reread and digest over the midwinter.

I am finding it hard to distinguish between birth and death, beginnings and endings, right now, so I looked them up in the dictionary; I go to my head and the safety of the intellect when fear is close at hand. The dictionary never fails. At birth our mothers bear us. Thinking about it, after death the earth bears us, or, at least, our remains. The 'th' of the words birth and death denote, apparently, a word which is a process. Quite a few wondrous words end in 'th', now I care to notice: aftermath, myth, oath, sooth, betroth, bequeath, growth, earth. I like that the word earth denotes a process: 'earthing'? I am reminded of my friends who have died and how their return to the earth will give rise to new life in the next round of things. On and on it goes, the cycle of life.

The other memory that absolutely refuses to budge as I write this article is reading the magazine, which came with the Sunday paper in my teenage years—I'm guessing I would have been about 12 or 13 and it was The Sunday Times magazine. It was an article documenting the changes in operations on foetuses and very young babies and how it was only recently that anaesthetics were used in these procedures. I remember my incredulity that clever people like doctors wouldn't have known or guessed that foetuses or babies feel pain. I think I even went and found my Mum to check whether this was actually the case (she was horrified too.) I can't get that memory out of my head. Interesting words—my poor head was so battered and bruised by my own tumultuous birth and rocky arrival here—not to mention my poor, long-suffering Mum, who was in shock following her Dad's very recent, sudden death. As a girl, I was terribly reluctant to join the world of grown ups - with the exception of grown ups like Roy and Winifred. This memory throws one light on why this was the case.

> As we move through life we continue to change and grow. But events such as birth and weaning, which until now have been viewed as 'object', physiological phenomena, produce definite and longlasting effects on the personality of a child. We must learn how to make the most of these opportunities (Verny with Kelly, 1982, 116).

I hadn't planned to write this final piece in a whatever-emerges-next sort of way. It's unnerving. I had planned an interesting article exploring neo-Reichian character structure (you'll know by now I'm a Reich fan!); voyaging into the patterns and character with birth at its heart—the boundary character, more traditionally known as the schizoid character. I wanted to explore how boundary character defences and patterning intrapsychically and relationally interact with the other character positions, which can shape us and our clients at the key stages of feeding, trying out our independence, time tabling, coming into relationship with our sex and gender, and our emerging wilfulness (see Kamalamani, 2012). But it wasn't to be; hopefully another time.

As this draws to a close, I'm laughing at myself—Zen style—because it feels like this piece of writing might be one of those pieces that never quite made it off the ground; a bit like my feeble attempts at making paper airplanes, let alone more sophisticated forms of origami. It puts me in mind of some of the great Mahayanan sutras of Buddhism; the White Lotus sutra comes to mind (see Soothill, 1987). These sutras are incredibly flowery and abundant; there is much praise for the wisdom and insight of the truth displayed in the sutra's verses, with repetitive verses and ornate surroundings, populated by billions of beings of shapes and sizes—lots of detail so that it is easy to miss what the sutra is actually saying.

Well, I'm not comfortable comparing my writing to a Buddhist sutra (!) but in the meantime, I have finally got around to the project I set myself, the night of Roy's funeral, which is to translate or adapt the words of St Teresa of Avila into non-God language. I've got nothing against God or those who worship him; it's just that life itself is my God (and I hope St Teresa forgives my poetic license).

> Let nothing disturb you,
> Let nothing frighten you,
> All things are passing:
> Life constantly changing.
> Practise patiently.
> Whoever knows life lacks nothing;
> Life alone prevails.

I want to thank dear Nancy, editor of *Somatic Psychotherapy Today*, for her invitation to write for this excellent publication five years ago. It has been a fabulous experience to be part of this project and to get to know you through this working relationship, as well as to read words of wisdom from the rest of you writing and contributing. A big, heartfelt thank you.

References:
Chamberlain, D. (1998). *The Mind of your Newborn Baby.* Berkeley, CA: North Atlantic Books.
Kamalamani. (2012). *Meditating with Character*. Mantra Books, an imprint of John Hunt Publishing, Hampshire, England. See chapter 6 for an introduction to post-Reichian character positions.
Maret, S.M. (1997). *The Prenatal Person: Frank Lake's Maternal-Fetal Distress Syndrome.*
Lanham, Maryland: University Press of America.
Márquez, G. G. (2007). *Love in the Time of Cholera.* London, England: Penguin Classics.
Soothill, W. E. (1987). *The Lotus of the Wonderful Law or the Lotus Gospel.* Richmond, Surrey:
Curzon Press Ltd.
Verny, T., & Kelly, J. (1982). *The Secret Life of the Unborn Child: A Remarkable and Controversial Look at Life Before Birth.* London, England: Sphere Publishing, an imprint of Little, Brown Book Group.

Web reference:
SPCK: http://spckpublishing.co.uk/blog/spckprayer/prayers-of-st-teresa-of-avila-1515-1582/ accessed 18/11/16.

About the Author

Kamalamani is a body psychotherapist, ecopsychologist, supervisor and facilitator with an interest in how therapy is shaped by its social, political, ecological and cultural context, drawing upon her experiences of being a development worker in sub-Saharan Africa, a lecturer in International Development at the University of Bristol, her current meditation practice and being a child lost and found in nature. Having practised Buddhist since 1995 she is also curious about the interface between therapy and Buddhism. Previously a steering group member of Psychotherapist and Counsellors for Social Responsibility, Kamalamani was also editor of *Transformations*. In addition to several journal articles she has written two books: *Meditating with Character* and *Other than Mother: Choosing Childlessness with Life in Mind* and is currently working on her third. She facilitates ecopsychology and Wild Therapy workshops and retreats.

info@kamalamani.co.uk
www.kamalamani.co.uk

About Somatic Psychotherapy Today

Somatic Psychotherapy Today offers a collection of articles and insights written to explore the relational realities in body oriented psychotherapy practices. The founding editor, Nancy Eichhorn, culls cutting edge theories and modalities in the somatic sciences to share with a worldwide audience while also providing a forum for sharing news and advances in clinical practice, research, resources, and policy. Information about professional activities and opportunities in the field of body oriented psychotherapies are offered as well.

SPT was founded in 2011 on the belief of the power of personal presence in a community of acceptance. What we do individually has a collective impact on our world – its health and wellbeing – and on all living entities that dwell here. Voicing our truth is paramount and finding the right venue to speak is just as critical. SPT offers writers and readers the space to connect, to share thoughts, ideas, and opinions about what matters in the work we do to further our field of study and practice.

While this publication cannot capture everything related to the immense field of psychotherapy and body oriented practices, we strive to provide a venue for our readers (be it therapists, students, researchers, folks in waiting rooms) to experience different perspectives in a light and lively manner we call educational entertainment.

SPT is an independent international publication that is validated by professional organizations and associations representing various modalities in the fields of body psychotherapy, somatic psychology, and prenatal and perinatal psychology.

Somatic Psychotherapy Today is currently a free magazine available on our website and at www.USABP.org www.EABP.org and www.issuu.com/SomaticPsychotherapyToday